5,00

The Morni

MW00512079

Vol. 5 ◆ JOURNAL ◆ No. 4

© 1996 by MorningStar Publications, Inc. All Rights Reserved.

Editor: Rick Joyner
Contributing Editors: Jack Deere, Francis Frangipane and Dudley Hall
General Editor: Steve Thompson
Managing Editor: Dianne C. Thomas
Production Manager: Mike Chaille
Production Assistants: Roger Hedgspeth, Scott Sheppard
Copy Editors: Becky Chaille, Terri Herrera

The Morning Star Journal is published quarterly, 4 issues per year, by MorningStar Publications, Inc., 16000 Lancaster Hwy, Charlotte, NC 28277-2061. Fall -1995 issue. Second-class postage, Charlotte, NC and additional mailing offices, 10832122 - ISSN.

POSTMASTER: Send address corrections to *The Morning Star Journal*, 16000 Lancaster Hwy, Charlotte, NC 28277-2061.
Subscription Rates: One year $12.95. Outside U.S. $20.00.

MorningStar Publications is a non-profit organization dedicated to the promulgation of important teachings and timely prophetic messages to the church. We also attempt to promote interchange between the different streams, emphases and denominations in the body of Christ.

To receive a subscription to *The Morning Star Journal*, send payment along with your name and address to MorningStar Publications, 16000 Lancaster Hwy, Charlotte, NC 28277-2061, (704) 542-0278 (1-800-542-0278—**Orders only**); FAX (704) 542-0280. One year (4 quarterly issues) U.S. $12.95; outside U.S. $20.00. Prices are subject to change without notice.

Reprints. Photocopies of any part of the contents of this publication may be made freely. However, to re-typeset information, permission must be requested in writing from MorningStar Publications, 16000 Lancaster Hwy, Charlotte, NC 28277-2061.

In this Journal NAS refers to the New American Standard Bible, copyright © 1960, 1962, 1963, 1968, 1971, 1973, 1974, 1977, by The Lockman Foundation. NKJV refers to the Holy Bible, New King James Version, © 1979, 1980, 1982 by Thomas Nelson, Inc. NIV refers to Holy Bible: New International Version ®, NIV®, © 1973, 1978, 1984 by International Bible Society. AMP refers to The Amplified Bible, © 1954, 1958, 1962, 1964, 1965 by Zondervan Publishing House. RSV refers to The Revised Standard Version, © 1962 by The World Publishing Co. TLB refers to The Living Bible © 1971 by Tyndale House Publishers. ASV refers to the American Standard Version. Italics in Scripture references are for emphasis only.

TRUE FOUNDATIONS

by

Rick Joyner

All Scripture references NAS unless otherwise indicated.

> **Therefore leaving the elementary teaching about the Christ, let us press on to maturity, not laying again a foundation of repentance from dead works and of faith toward God,**
>
> **of instruction about washings, and laying on of hands, and the resurrection of the dead, and eternal judgment (Hebrews 6:1-2).**

Here we are encouraged to **"not lay again a foundation of repentance."** However, it is understood that this exhortation is for those who have properly laid a foundation of repentance from dead works. It is weakness in this part of the foundation of Christianity that is the source for much of the deception and defeat that prevails over the modern church. Repentance is a factor that will determine the true quality and depth of our spiritual life. John the Baptist had to preach repentance before Jesus could be revealed. Without repentance the people would not have been able to recognize the Messiah, much less properly relate to Him. Repentance is a foundation of the true Christian life. Until the guilt of our sin becomes too unbearable and weighty for us to carry, we simply will not turn to the cross. Repentance is the confession of failure and the cry for help. Therefore repentance is the evidence of spiritual humility, and God only gives His grace to the humble (see James 4:6).

Human philosophies have offered many reliefs from guilt, and many of them will temporarily relieve the symptoms of our deadly spiritual disease, but the cross alone can cure us. When we try to relieve the symptoms of sin, such as guilt and depression, without confronting the cause of those symptoms, we only cover up this cancer so that it can grow unhindered. The cross uses the symptoms to lead us to the disease, and then it delivers us from the guilt and depression by killing the disease. Jesus did not just come to save us from death or hell; He came to save us from what is causing the death and hell.

Foundations Are Important

As Steve Thompson pointed out in one of our local pastors' meetings, there have been studies made that indicate a strong link between the nature of the birth and the course of the child's life. For example, when the philosophy of childbirth was promulgated that has been called, "drug them and tug them," which was to drug the mother and pull the baby out, the first generation born by the widespread use of this procedure became the first to widely use drugs. Such studies are general and do not apply to every individual, but overall the trends are obvious.

This principle, that has been found to be true in the natural, is also true in relation to spiritual births. Those who are born into the kingdom through a radical conviction of sin, through great and difficult travail over their spiritual condition and the need for salvation, with but a few exceptions, are the strongest, most radical and most effective Christians. Likewise, those who are born again as the result of a weak gospel message tend to be weak and perpetually in need of ministry.

The Shackles of Sin

One may ask, how can we help the conditions under which we were born? It is true that we had nothing to do with the quality of the message preached that brought us into the kingdom. We had nothing to do with the state of the church, our mother. In a sense, she has been using spiritual "drugs" to make the birth process as painless as possible. These drugs are the doctrines of delusion that we are subject to when we are more concerned about feeling good than knowing the truth. But obviously if we were born into the church while she was in this state, we could not help it. So why are we being condemned for what we were not in control of? The apostle Paul succinctly answered this question, **"The thing molded will not say to the molder, 'Why did you make me like this,' will it?" (Romans 9:20).** This may be a valid question, maybe even an excuse, but to use it only strengthens the shackles of our sin.

The first result of the first sin was self-centeredness—Adam and Eve looked at themselves and saw that they were naked. The next result was blame-shifting. Adam blamed the woman, which God had given to Him, effectively putting the blame back on God for his sin. The woman blamed the serpent for her sin, and since God was the one who allowed it in the Garden, it must all be His fault, thus relieving her of any responsibility. Such excuses may make us feel better about ourselves for a time, but they make our deliverance from the problem impossible. The recovery of personal responsibility is the first step that must be taken for salvation to come. God does not forgive excuses; He forgives sin. The first evidence that true salvation is working in us is that we stop looking at ourselves and start looking at God. The second evidence is that we stop blaming everyone else for our problems and start confessing them as sins.

It is true that we may have had nothing to do with the condition of our birth. We did not choose to be born into this world in such a fallen condition. We can stand on this fact to our eternal dismay, or we can seize the salvation that has so graciously been provided for us. We may want to blame our potty training for all of our problems. We can blame parents, teachers, brothers, sisters, or other Christians for our problems, and it may be true that we may have suffered injustices from all of them. There may be genuine reasons for us to be the way we are. We can hang onto our excuses, and our sin, or we can be freed, and be made into new creatures who bear the glorious image of Christ. But we will never be freed until we take our eyes off of ourselves and look to Him, and stop blame-shifting and confess our own sins.

A great grace is coming that is going to allow many who have been both improperly born and raised spiritually to rebuild their foundations. This does not mean that everything in their spiritual experience must be thrown out, or is useless, but a great renewal is coming to strengthen the whole body of Christ by replacing delusions with the power of the cross. This can only be done on the true foundation of repentance. Once a foundation is laid, it is not that we do not use it again, but rather the whole building can only stand as long as it remains strong. We do not lay the foundation again in the sense that we do not put a foundation on top of the second or third stories, but the foundation is used every day that the building is used. We never stop repenting when we need to, but once a strong and clear understanding of it becomes a part of our life, we do not need to keep teaching it, or laying again that foundation.

Pain Is a Friend

A good conscience that pangs us with guilt is one of the most needed ingredients for a healthy spiritual life. Such a conscience is really a sensitivity to the Holy Spirit. One of His primary duties is to convict of sin. Those who are no longer convicted by their sin are in the most dangerous condition of having a seared conscience that no longer responds to the Holy Spirit.

It is easy to understand how modern medicine would want to relieve pain that is deemed unnecessary. Even human compassion is moved to do all that it can to remove pain from the world. However, pain has a most important place in the present state of the world, and to alleviate it can be very dangerous. As the proverb states, **"Faithful are the wounds of a friend, but deceitful are the kisses of an enemy" (Proverbs 27:6).** Pain is an alarm that something is wrong and needs correction. It is the shallowness of our present state that has made pain the enemy. Pain is a friend that is trying to warn us about the real problem.

Spiritual pain is caused by the conviction of sin. Freud was right when he discerned that guilt was the cause of most of the depression and neurosis afflicting the world. However, he possibly released more depression and neurosis upon the world than any other single person when he began attacking the guilt instead of the cause of the guilt—sin! If we remove the guilt before the sin is removed it is like relieving a headache that is caused by brain cancer—then the tumor can grow undetected until it is too late.

We are guilty, and it is right that we feel guilt until we have been to the cross to have it relieved. I am not okay and you are not okay. We are in desperate need of help, and the cross is the only place that we can find it. The cross is the power of God, it is the only provision for true salvation, deliverance or healing. If we are to know the power of God in our daily lives, we must take up our crosses daily. Going to the cross is painful, but it is the only place where the pain can truly be relieved. Once we have been crucified with Christ there is no greater freedom from pain that we can know. It must be our goal as Christians to relieve the guilt and pain, not by removing the symptoms, but by removing that which is causing them—sin.

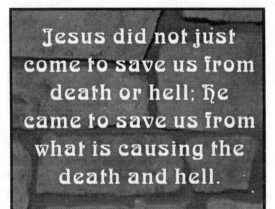

Jesus did not just come to save us from death or hell; He came to save us from what is causing the death and hell.

The reality with which we face our sin in the beginning of our Christian life will almost certainly dictate the reality with which we will face our entire lives. That reality will have much to do with the degree of truth that we walk in. I did not say the degree of truth that we *know*, but the degree of truth that we *walk in*. The basic definition of a hypocrite is one who knows the truth but does not live it. The Lord reserved His most scathing condemnation for the hypocrites because that is the most dangerous state that we can be in.

A Barometer of Our Condition

There is reason to both rejoice and be sobered by the testimonies of healing and deliverance of those who have been touched by the present move of the Spirit popularly known as "the Toronto blessing." However, we should be sobered by the fact that so many Christians, who have been in the faith for numerous years, still needed such deliverance. Many of the testimonies of deliverance from depression, bitterness, hatreds, etc., were from men and women who have been Christians for twenty or thirty years! Why is it taking so long to receive deliverance from those things that we should have been freed of when we were born again? When we are born again, **"all things are become new" (II Corinthians 5:17 KJV).** If all things have become new there is no longer a reason to feel rejected or resentful about our past. How can we who have been given such a glorious future in Christ, eternal life in the splendors of heaven, who have been given angels as ministers, be so concerned about such pettiness in this temporary realm? It can only be because we are still earthly-minded, which the apostle explained would only result in death (see Romans 8:6). Why do we still choose death over life? Why do we go on eating from the Tree of the Knowledge of Good and Evil when the Tree of Life is available to us?

It is right to rejoice when anyone is delivered from the fruit and shackles of sin such as bitterness or depression, but we must also be sobered by the fact that we need so much of it. The church is, generally, in a very low state. The ultimate vision of many is to just get to the place where a new Christian should be walking from the time they are born again. We are called to be a "new creation" that greatly exceeds the original creation before the fall. We have been given something much greater than just walking with God in the Garden, or even walking with Jesus when He walked upon the earth—we have Him living inside of us! The same power that created the universe is in even the youngest Christian. If just one Christian starts to walk in the reality of what we have been given, the whole world will be shocked into soberness, quickly. As the apostle Paul stated it:

But if the ministry of death, in letters engraved on stones, came with glory, so that the sons of Israel could not look intently at the face of Moses because of the glory of his face, fading as it was,

how shall the ministry of the Spirit fail to be even more with glory? (II Corinthians 3:7-8).

Paul is clearly saying that normal, New Covenant ministry should come with even more glory than Moses experienced, and he had to put a veil over his face because it was so great. Where is the glory in the church? Who could claim to have experienced even the glory that Moses did? This obviously indicates that there is much more available than we are presently walking in. Our goal should be much more than just having healthy, happy lives. We are called to be bearers of the glory of God. We are called to challenge even the greatest

darkness of our times, and push it back. We are here to tear down the enemy's strongholds, and set the captives free. All that is now happening is wonderful, but we must never lose the vision for something that is much greater than anything that we are yet seeing. As Bonnie Chavda observed, the purpose of the cup bearer was to get Joseph out of prison. Learning to drink the wine of the Spirit is important, but we must not camp here, we must keep going higher. Let us never stop praying what has become one of the great prophetic prayers of our times—MORE LORD!

The present renewal movement is not taking the church to new ground, but it is helping multitudes of believers take back ground that has been lost. It is already a movement of historic significance, but it is also apparently beginning to peak and subside. This is not a defeat, but a sign that the job has been done. It is now time to go forward. Once the army is healed it must march. If we do not go on to higher ground, we will sink back to an even lower state. But that will only happen if we refuse to hear the clear trumpet call that is already being sounded.

The bride of the Lamb is **"as awesome as an army with banners" (Song of Solomon 6:4).** The banners of her great companies are now being unfurled all over the earth. When she begins to march again the earth will tremble at the sound of it. Let us not be left behind. Regardless of how you may have been hurt by church relationships in the past, get healed and get back in the ranks. The awesome day of the Lord is very near. ∎

A SERVANT, *OR A FRIEND*?

by ——
Bob Sorge

All Scripture references NKJV unless otherwise indicated.

The Lord is reorienting how I relate to the Father. I have been seeking the Lord most fervently for a physical healing for almost three years now, and the Lord has been showing me recently that I have had an immature concept of how to relate to God.

I have approached prayer as the way to get from God what I want (which in my case has been a healing). I imagined it something like this: if I responded properly to all His dealings, and had the right kind of faith, God would then be able to heal me. I saw it like the pins of a lock—once all the pins of the lock were properly engaged, the lock would snap open, and I would be healed. So the key to divine healing, in my mind, was getting everything right all at once.

But there are a couple things wrong with this picture. First, it paints the Father as a somewhat reluctant giver who will not dispense grace until everything is in order. But if God's grace were given to me only when I responded correctly, I would never have any grace on my life! Second, this skewed picture suggests that my job is to "jump through heaven's hoops" so that I can extract from heaven what I want.

The Lord has "called me higher" to relate to Him on a different level altogether. Instead of me being the supplicant and Him being the supplier, the Lord wants me to come to a "workers together" mentality (see I Corinthians 3:9). I am to share His heart so completely that His desires become my desires, His plans become my plans, and His work becomes my work. He wants me to be His partner, someone who so fully shares the pulsations of His heart that my life becomes an extension of His will and purpose on the earth.

When I enter this dimension in its fullness, I will see that God wants me to be healed as much or more than I do. My preoccupation, then, ceases to be "prevailing prayer." That term carries the idea that my task in prayer is to convince God to supply what I want. Instead, the Lord is calling me to "cooperative prayer." In cooperative prayer, I become the vehicle on earth to birth through intercession the perfect will of God in heaven.

The fully mature partner of the Lord Jesus moves in parallel motion with heaven. He waits upon God until he perceives the heart of the Father, and then he works on earth in the power of the Spirit to be a catalyst for God's purposes to be accomplished here in space and time. Rather than trying to extract his agenda from God, he is now learning to be a cooperative enforcer of God's agenda on earth.

This dimension of life in the Spirit is called "friendship with God." Look carefully at these words of Jesus:

> **Greater love has no one than this, than to lay down one's life for his friends.**
> **You are My friends if you do whatever I command you. No longer do I call you servants, for a servant does not know what his master is doing;**
> **but I have called you friends, for all things that I heard from My Father I Have made known to you (John 15:13-15).**

Friendship with God

I have been in full-time ministry for almost fourteen years, and have been, to the best of my ability, a faithful servant of Jesus. I have worked hard for Him, have watched His blessings attend my life, and have had the joy of furthering His kingdom. But I am seeing that there is a level of relationship with Jesus that is higher than servanthood, and it is that of friendship. Oh! to be a friend of God!

Based upon these words of Jesus, I would like to suggest several distinctions between a servant and a friend:

* The Lord always begins in our lives by calling us to servanthood. Everyone starts off as a servant. It is a glorious attainment when we become fully surrendered in heart, mind, soul and body to the Lord.

* A servant is like an employee; a friend is brought into management and made a co-owner. Then we can truly say "I am a bondslave of Jesus Christ." Sadly enough, few attain this level of surrender, and even fewer become friends.

* A servant can be deployed anywhere there's a need—the Master has many menial tasks that need to be done. But a friend is allowed to work in those areas that are most significant in the eyes of the Master.

* A friend prays differently than a servant. A servant desires to move the hand of God; a friend desires to know the heart of God. A friend won't harangue God with his own requests, but will hold his tongue until he knows the mind of the Spirit. A servant prays for the blessings he desires, but a friend seeks to be an intercessor through whom heaven's will can come to earth.

* A servant does his utmost to use his own best judgment to further the

interests of the Master. A friend has come to know the Master personally, so he is able to further the interests of the Master in the same way that the Master Himself would if He were there.

* The issue for a servant is faithfulness (see Matthew 25:21); the issue for a friend is love (see John 15:13). Martha served Jesus faithfully, but Mary loved Him. A servant is willing to work for the Master, a friend wants to be with the Master. It's a more demanding commitment to be a friend than a servant. A friendship requires investment of energy and time. In one sense it's easier to keep it at the Master/servant level. The friend and the servant both work for the Master, but after the work is done, the servant goes about his own business whereas the friend sits down with the Master.

* The most gripping distinction of all is made by Jesus Himself in the passage cited above. Jesus said that a servant just does what he's told, without necessarily understanding why he's doing what he's doing. But a friend is confided in. A friend is told the thoughts and intentions behind the plan of action. To say it precisely, Jesus confides His purposes to His friends.

* Jesus made it clear that the pathway to friendship is through implicit obedience. **"You are My friends if you do whatever I command you" (John 15:14).** In the absence of a directive, a servant will use his best judgment; but a friend will wait until a directive comes. Thus, the discipline of waiting for the Master's directive is vital to becoming His friend. What is to be done when circumstances scream for immediate action, but no word from God has come? This is the fiery test of the servant of God. If he will wait—even past the deadline if need be—he will learn something about friendship with God.

Vision Versus Purpose

I have been a man of vision. I have established goals for myself each year, and have urged the leaders in our church to do likewise. Most books on Christian leadership deal to one degree or another with the necessity of establishing vision, setting goals, and learning how to evaluate the progress toward those goals.

We adopt a vision for our ministry for this year, and for the next five years, and for the next ten years. We develop a Vision Statement and a Mission Statement. We brainstorm what exploits we might accomplish for God's kingdom. We are visionary leaders.

Looking at how few Prophets there are and seeing how the Church treats the few there are, it's no wonder the Church is a nonprophet organization.
Warren W. Wiersbe

With only one slight problem: God doesn't operate out of vision. He doesn't have a vision for your life or for your ministry, and He doesn't have a vision for this planet. God only has purpose. He has a purpose for your life, and for the entire human race, and His purposes will be accomplished.

As I speak of "vision" in this sense, I am speaking of that forward-looking hope of future progress. Vision is hopeful, purpose is as good as done. God does not merely "hope" that His plans will be fulfilled, for He has determined *a priori* that they will be accomplished. Now, God does impart vision to us (see Habakkuk 2:2), but it is always in conformity with His purpose. In other words, a true vision from God is certain to be fulfilled, for it is the purpose of God revealed in advance. Much of the time, when we think we're operating out of godly vision, we're merely working in human creativity. This is evidenced by the sheer volume of goals that we've never achieved.

We're reduced to being visionary when we don't know God's purposes. After getting a general sense of the game plan, servants develop a vision of what they can do for God; a friend, on the other hand, is God's confidant who hears His heart and perceives His purposes for his life and ministry.

God doesn't ask us to be creative, but to be obedient. Sometimes the creativity of Christian leaders does damage to the kingdom of God, because we mobilize believers in efforts that didn't originate in the heart of God. The way of God is this: "Wait on Me, until I speak to you."

I've discovered that it's much easier to be creative than obedient, because creativity requires planning but obedience requires listening. It's easier to plan than to listen. Sometimes I can come up with ten great ideas before God says anything!

A servant operates in the vision of what could be; a friend operates in the confidence of what will be. A friend of God will accomplish far more, for he will not muddy the waters with his own creative juices. Instead of getting in God's way, he will get in God's Ways.

The Ways of God

Here's the amazing part: When you begin to hear God's ideas and to act upon them, others will be astounded at your "creativity." The reason is simply because God's thoughts and ways are so different from ours (see Isaiah 55:8-9), that when He begins to reveal His purposes to us they will be strikingly extraordinary. One way to know it's God's idea is that you would have never come up with that idea on your own.

God's ways will always be different from your ways. You can get frustrated with that, or you can choose to be attracted by that. (God made us to be naturally attracted to that which is different from ourselves.) Personally, I'm fascinated by His ways. The fact that I do not understand His ways fuels my desire to know Him better.

If we're all called to be obedient rather than creative, can you understand how this puts us all at the same level? The naturally creative person has no advantage over the one who feels like a creative dullard. We're all reduced to this one common denominator: We must hear from God. There is great liberty here for those who will receive it.

Paul wrote in Ephesians 3:20, **"Now to Him who is able to do exceedingly abundantly above all that we ask or think, according to the power that works in us"**—There is a power in me that far exceeds my thinking. There is a power in me that far exceeds my imagination. So why limit what God wants to do in my life to my own creative thinking? I'm going to dispense with my own ingenuity, and tune into what He wants to do by His incredible power which resides in and flows through me.

Paul continued, **"To Him be glory in the church by Christ Jesus to all generations, forever and ever. Amen"** **(Ephesians 3:21).** My ideas leave a way of directing a certain percentage of attention to myself; His ideas redound only to His glory. That makes His ideas not only better, but safe.

Understanding His Purposes

Abraham was called the friend of God (see James 2:23). He wasn't a man of vision, he was a man to whom God revealed His purposes (see Genesis 18:17-21). It was because of his understanding of God's purposes that Abraham was able to offer his son as a sacrifice to God.

You don't just decide you're going to become somebody's best friend. Friendship is something that must "click." There must be a compatibility of personality, of interests, a certain "chemistry" that makes a friendship a mutually meaningful relationship. God isn't the friend of some of us because He simply can't relate to us. He knows we love Him, but we're so self-absorbed that we keep ourselves at servant level.

"How can I change?" someone might ask. We do not initiate this change. We are drawn into friendship by the compelling overtures of the Holy Spirit. As the Holy Spirit reveals to us what it means to be a friend of the almighty God of the universe, a prayer begins to arise in our hearts, "Lord, plant my feet on higher ground." You cannot plant yourself on higher ground, you can only cry for Him to draw you. He places the cry in your heart, and He draws you—from beginning to end, it is all of Him.

In the final analysis, the chief preoccupation of friends is simply this: to delight in each other. ■

BOB SORGE is pastor of Zion Fellowship in Canandaigua, NY. He served for three years as Director of Music at Elim Bible Institute, Lima, NY where he established a training program for worship leaders. Author of the widely acclaimed book, **EXPLORING WORSHIP**, Bob has just written another book, **IN HIS FACE: A PROPHETIC CALL TO RENEWED FOCUS** (available through Christian bookstores). Bob and his wife, Marci, enjoy serving the Lord in Canandaigua, where they reside with their three children.

THE ALMOST CHRISTIAN

by George Whitfield

All Scripture references KJV unless otherwise indicated.

Almost thou persuadest me to be a Christian **(Acts 26:28).**

These words contain the ingenuous confession of King Agrippa which, having some reference to the preceding verses, it may not be improper to relate the substance of them.

The chapter out of which the text is taken contains an admirable account which the great St. Paul gave of his wonderful conversion from Judaism to Christianity, when he was called to make his defense before Festus, a Gentile governor, and King Agrippa. Our blessed Lord had long since foretold that when the Son of man should be lifted up, His disciples would be brought before the kings and rulers, for His name's sake, for a testimony unto them (see Matthew 10:18; Mark 13:9). And very good was the design of Infinite Wisdom in thus ordaining it. For Christianity, being from the beginning a doctrine of the cross, the princes and rulers of the earth thought themselves too high to be instructed by such mean teachers, or too happy to be disturbed by such unwelcome truths; and therefore would have always continued strangers to Jesus Christ and Him crucified, had not the apostles, by being arraigned before them, gained opportunities of preaching to them Jesus and the resurrection.

St. Paul knew full well that this was the main reason why his blessed Master permitted his enemies at this time to arraign him in a public court; and, therefore, in compliance with the divine will, thought it not sufficient barely to make his defense, but endeavored at the same time to convert his judges (Acts 26:24-28). And this he did with such demonstration of the Spirit and of power that Festus, unwilling to be convinced by the strongest evidence, cried out with a loud voice, **"Paul, much learning doth make thee mad."** To which the brave apostle (like a true follower of the holy Jesus) meekly replied, **"I am not mad, most noble Festus; but speak forth the words of truth and soberness."**

In all probability, seeing King Agrippa more affected with his discourse, and observing in him an inclination to know the truth, he applied himself more particularly to him. **"The king knoweth of these things, before whom also I speak freely: for I am persuaded that none of these things are hidden from him."** And then, that if possible he might complete his wished-for conversion, he, with an inimitable strain of oratory, addressed himself still more closely, **"King Agrippa, believest thou the prophets? I know that thou believest them."** At which the passions of the king began to work so strongly, that he was obliged in open court to own himself affected by the prisoner's preaching, and ingenuously to cry out, **"Paul, Almost thou persuadest me to be a Christian."**

These words, taken with the context, afford us a lively representation of the different reception which the doctrine of Christ's ministers, who come in the power and spirit of Paul, meets with nowadays in the minds of men. For notwithstanding they, like this great apostle, **"speak forth the words of truth and soberness,"** and with such energy and power that all their adversaries cannot justly gainsay or resist; yet, too many, with the noble Festus before mentioned, being, like him, either too proud to be taught, or too sensual, too careless, or too worldly-minded to live up to the doctrine, in order to excuse themselves, cry out that "much learning [much study, or, what is more unaccountable, much piety] hath made thee mad." And though, blessed be God! All

do not thus disbelieve our report, yet amongst those who gladly receive the Word, and confess that we speak the words of truth and soberness, there are so few who arrive at any higher degree of piety than that of Agrippa, or are any farther persuaded than to be almost Christians, that I cannot but think it highly necessary to warn them of the danger of such a state. And therefore, from the words of the text, shall endeavor to show three things:

First, what is meant by an almost Christian.

An almost Christian, if we consider him in respect to his duty to God, is one that halts between two opinions; that wavers between Christ and the world; that would reconcile God and mammon, light and darkness, Christ and Belial. It is true, he has an inclination to religion, but then he is very cautious lest he goes too far in it; his false heart is always crying out, "Spare thyself, do thyself no harm." He prays that God's will may be done on earth, as it is in heaven. But notwithstanding, he is very partial in his obedience, and fondly hopes that God will not be extreme to mark everything

that he willfully does amiss, though an inspired apostle has told him, "he who offends in one point is guilty of all." But chiefly, he is one that depends much on outward ordinances, and on that account looks upon himself as righteous, and despises others; though at the same time he is as great a stranger to the divine life as any other person whatsoever. In short, he is fond of the form, but never experiences the power of godliness in his heart. He goes on year after year, attending on the means of grace, but, like Pharaoh's lean kine, he is never the better, but rather the worse for it.

If you consider him in respect to his neighbor, he is one that is strictly just to all; but then this does not proceed from any love to God or regard to man, but only through a principle of self-love, because he knows dishonesty will spoil his reputation, and consequently hinder his thriving in the world.

He is one that depends much upon being negatively good, and contents himself with the consciousness of having done no one any harm, though he reads in the gospel that the unprofitable servant was cast into outer darkness (see Matthew 25:14-30), and the barren fig tree was cursed and dried up from the roots, for bearing not bad fruit, but no fruit (see Mark 11:12-21).

He is no enemy to charitable contributions in public, if not too frequently recommended: but then he is unacquainted with the kind offices of visiting the sick and imprisoned, clothing the naked and relieving the hungry in a personal manner. He thinks that these things belong only to the clergy, though

his own false heart tells him that nothing but pride keeps him from exercising these acts of humility; and that Jesus Christ condemns persons to everlasting punishment, not merely for being fornicators, drunkards, or extortioners, but for neglecting these charitable offices:

When the Son of man shall come in his glory

he shall set the sheep on his right hand, but the goats on the left

Then shall he say also unto them on the left hand, Depart from me, ye cursed, into everlasting fire, prepared for the devil and his angels:

for I was an hungered, and ye gave me no meat; I was thirsty, and ye gave me no drink:

I was a stranger, and ye took me not in: naked, and ye clothed me not: sick, and in prison, and ye visited me not.

Then shall they also answer him, saying, Lord, when saw we thee an hungered, or athirst, or a stranger, or naked, or sick, or in prison, and did not minister unto thee?

Then shall he answer them, saying, Verily I say unto you, Inasmuch as ye did it not to one of the least of these, ye did it not to me.

And these shall go away into everlasting punishment (Matthew 25:31, 33, 41-46).

I thought it proper to give you this whole passage of Scripture, because our Savior lays such a particular stress upon it; and yet it is so little regarded, that were we to judge by the practice of Christians, we would be tempted to think there were no such verses in the Bible.

To proceed to the character of an almost Christian. If we consider him in respect of himself, as we said, he is strictly honest to his neighbor, so he is likewise strictly sober in himself; but then both dishonesty and sobriety proceed from the same principle of a false self-love. It is true, he runs not into the same excess of riot with other men; but then it is not out of obedience to the laws of God, but either because his constitution dislikes intemperance; or rather because he is cautious of forfeiting his reputation, or unfitting himself for temporal business. But though he is so prudent as to avoid intemperance and excess, for the reasons before mentioned, yet he always goes to the extremity of what is lawful. It is true, he is no drunkard; but then he has no Christian self-denial. He cannot think our Savior to be so austere a Master, as to deny us to indulge ourselves in some particulars: and so by this means he is destitute of a sense of true religion, as much as if he lived in debauchery, or any other crime whatever. As to settling his principles as well as practice, he is guided more by the world than by the word of God: for his part, he cannot think the way to heaven so narrow as some would make it; and therefore considers not so much what Scripture requires, as what such and such a good man does, or what will best suit his own corrupt inclinations. Upon this account he is not only very cautious himself, but

likewise very careful of young converts, whose faces are set heavenward; and therefore is always acting the devil's part, and bidding them spare themselves, though they are doing no more than what the Scripture strictly requires them to do: the consequence of that is, that he suffers not himself to enter into the kingdom of God, and those that are entering in he hinders.

Thus lives the almost Christian; not that I can say I have fully described him to you, but from these outlines and sketches of his character, if your consciences have done their proper work, and made a particular application of what has been said to your own hearts, I cannot but fear that some of you may observe some features in his picture, odious as it is, too nearly resembling your own. Therefore I cannot but hope that you will join with the apostle in the words immediately following the text, and wish yourselves to be not only almost, but altogether Christians (see Acts 26:29).

Second, why so many are no more than almost Christians.

1. **The first reason I shall mention is, because so many set out with *false notions of religion*; though they live in a Christian country, they know not what Christianity is.** This perhaps may be esteemed a hard saying, but experience sadly evinces the truth of it; for some place religion as being of this or that communion; more, in morality; most, in a round of duties, and a

model of performances; and few, very few, acknowledge it to be what it really is, a thorough inward change of nature, a divine life, a vital participation of Jesus Christ, a union of the soul with God; which the apostle expressed by saying, **"He that is joined unto the Lord is one spirit" (I Corinthians 6:17).**

Hence it happens that so many, even of the most knowing professors, when you come to converse with them concerning the essence, the life, the soul of religion, I mean our new birth in Jesus Christ, confess themselves quite ignorant of the matter, and cry out with Nicodemus, **"How can these things be?" (John 3:9).** And no wonder then that so many are only almost Christians, when so many know not what Christianity is: no marvel that so many take up with the form, when they are quite strangers to the power of godliness; or content themselves with the shadow, when they know so little about the substance of it. And this is one cause why so many are almost, and so few are altogether Christians.

2. **A second reason that may be assigned why so many are no more than almost Christians, is** *a servile fear of man.* **Multitudes there are, and have been, who, though awakened to a sense of the divine life, and having tasted and felt the powers of the world to come; yet out of a base sinful fear of being counted singular, or**

despised by men, have allowed all those good impressions to wear off. It is true, they have some esteem for Jesus Christ, but then, like Nicodemus, they would come to him only by night. They are willing to serve Him, but then they would do it secretly, for fear of the Jews; they have a mind to see Jesus, but then they cannot come to Him because of the crowd, and for fear of being laughed at and ridiculed by those with whom they used to sit at meat.

Well did our Savior prophesy of such persons, **"How can ye believe, which receive honor one of another?" (John 5:44).** Have they never read that, **"The friendship of the world is enmity with God" (James 4:4).** and that our Lord himself has threatened, **"Whosoever therefore shall be ashamed of me and of my words in this adulterous and sinful generation; of him also shall the Son of man be ashamed, when he cometh in the glory of his Father, with the holy angels" (Mark 8:38)?** No wonder that so many are no more than almost Christians, since so many have **"loved the praise of men more than the praise of God" (John 12:45).**

3. **A third reason why so many are no more than almost Christians, is** *a reigning love of money.* **This** was the pitiable case of that forward young man in the Gospel who came running to our blessed Lord and, kneeling before him, inquired what he must do to inherit eternal life, to

whom our blessed Master replied, **"Thou knowest the commandments, Do not commit adultery, Do not kill, Do not steal,"** to which the young man replied, **"All these have I observed from my youth."** But when our Lord proceeded to tell him, **"One thing thou lackest: go thy way, sell whatsoever thou hast, and give to the poor,"** he was grieved at that saying, and went away sorrowful, **"for he had great possessions!" (Mark 10:19-22).**

Poor youth! He had a good mind to be a Christian, and to inherit eternal life, but thought it too dear, if it could be purchased at no less an expense than of his estate! And thus many, both young and old, nowadays come running to worship our Lord in public, and kneel before him in private, and inquire at his gospel, what they must do to inherit eternal life; but when they find they must renounce the self-enjoyment of riches, and forsake all in affection to follow him, they cry, "The Lord pardon us in this thing! We pray Thee have us excused" (see Luke 14:15-24).

But is heaven so small a trifle in men's esteem, as not to be worth a little gilded earth? Is eternal life so mean a purchase, as not to deserve a temporary renunciation of a few transitory riches? Surely it is. But however inconsistent such a behavior may be, this inordinate love of money is too evidently the common and fatal cause why so many are no more than almost Christians.

4. **Nor is *the love of pleasure* a less uncommon or a less fatal cause why so many are no more than almost Christians.** Thousands and ten thousands there are who despise riches and would willingly be true disciples of Jesus Christ, if parting with their money would make them so; but when they are told that our blessed Lord has said, **"If any man will come after me, let him deny himself" (Matthew 16:24),** like the pitiable young man before mentioned, they go away sorrowful, for they have too great love for sensual pleasures. They will perhaps send for the ministers of Christ, as Herod did for John, and hear them gladly, but touch them in their Herodias (see Luke 3:19-20), tell them they must part with such and such a darling pleasure, and with wicked Ahab they cry out, "Hast thou found us, O our enemy?" (see I Kings 21:20). Tell them of the necessity of mortification and self-denial, and it is as difficult for them to hear, as if you were to bid them, "Cut off a right hand or pluck out a right eye." They cannot think our Lord requires so much at their hands, though an inspired apostle has commanded us to "mortify our members which are upon earth" (see Colossians 3:5). And who himself, even after he had converted thousands, and had very nearly arrived at the end of his race, yet professed that it was his daily practice to, keep under his body, and bring it into subjection, lest, after he had preached to others, he

himself should be a castaway (see I Corinthians 9:27).

But some men would be wiser than this great apostle, and chalk out to us what they falsely imagine an easier way to happiness. They would flatter us that we may go to heaven without offering violence to our sensual appetites; and enter into the strait gate without striving against our carnal inclinations. And this is another reason why so many are only almost, and not altogether, Christians.

5. **The fifth and last reason I shall assign why so many are only almost Christians is** *a fickleness and instability of temper.*

It has been, no doubt, a misfortune that many a minister and sincere Christian has met with, weeping and wailing over numbers of promising converts, who seemingly began in the Spirit, but after a while fell away, and basely ended in the flesh; and this not for want of right notions in religion, nor out of a servile fear of man, nor from the love of money, or of sensual pleasure, but through an instability and fickleness of temper. They looked upon religion merely for novelty, as something which pleased them for a while; but after their curiosity was satisfied they laid it aside again: like the young man that came to see Jesus with a linen cloth about his naked body (see Mark 14:51), they have followed him for a season, but when temptations came to take hold on them, for want of a little more

resolution, they have been stripped of all their good intentions, and fled away naked.

They at first, like a tree planted by the water-side, grew up and flourished for a while; but having no root in themselves, no inward principle of holiness and piety, like Jonah's gourd, they were soon dried up and withered. Their good intentions are, too, like the violent motions of the animal spirits of a body newly beheaded, which, though impetuous, are not lasting. In short, they set out well in their journey to heaven, but finding the way either narrower or longer than they expected, through an unsteadiness of temper, they have made a halt, and so returned like the dog to his vomit, or like the sow that was washed to her wallowing in the mire.

I tremble to pronounce the fate of such unstable professors, who, having put their hands to the plow, for want of a little more resolution, shamefully look back. How shall I repeat to them that dreadful threatening, **"If any man draw back, my soul shall have no pleasure in him" (Hebrews 10:38),** and again, **"It is impossible for those who were once enlightened, and have tasted of the heavenly gift . . . and the powers of the world to come, if they should fall away, to renew them again unto repentance" (Hebrews 6:4-6).** But notwithstanding the gospel is so severe against apostates, yet many that began well, through a fickleness of temper (oh, that none of us may ever be such!), have been, by this means, of the number of those that turn back unto perdition.

Third, the folly of being no more than almost Christian.

1. **The first proof I shall give of the folly of such a proceeding is that it is ineffectual to salvation.** It is true, such men are almost good; but almost to hit the mark is really to miss it. God requires us, to love him with all our hearts, with all our souls, and with all our strength (see Matthew 22:37). He loves us too well to admit any rival; because, so far as our hearts are empty of God, so far must they be unhappy. The devil, indeed, like the false mother that came before Solomon, would have our hearts divided, as she would have had the child (see I Kings 3:16-28); but God, like the true mother, will have all or none. "My son, give me thy heart," thy whole heart, is the general call to all: and if this be not done, we never can expect the divine mercy.

Persons may play the hypocrite; but God at the great day will strike them dead (as he did Ananias and Sapphira by the mouth of his servant Peter, see Acts 5:1-11), for pretending to offer Him all their hearts, when they keep back from Him the greatest part. They may perhaps impose upon their fellow creatures for a while; but He that

enabled Ahijah to cry out, **"Come in, thou wife of Jeroboam" (I Kings 14:6),** when she came disguised to inquire about her sick son, will also discover them through their most artful dissimulations; and if their hearts are not wholly with Him, appoint them their portion with hypocrites and unbelievers.

2. **What renders a half-way piety more inexcusable is that it is not only insufficient to our own salvation, but also very prejudicial to that of others.**

An almost Christian is one of the most hurtful creatures in the world; he is a wolf in sheep's clothing. He is one of those false prophets our blessed Lord bids us beware of, in His Sermon on the Mount, who would persuade men that the way to heaven is broader than it really is; and thereby, as it was observed before, "enter not into the kingdom of God themselves; and those that are entering in they hinder." These are the men that turn the world into a lukewarm Laodicean spirit; that hang out false lights and so shipwreck unthinking benighted souls in their voyage to the haven of eternity. These are they who are greater enemies to the cross of Christ than infidels themselves: for of an unbeliever everyone will be aware, but an almost Christian, through his subtle hypocrisy, draws away many after him, and therefore must expect to receive the greater damnation.

3. **As it is most prejudicial to ourselves and hurtful to others, so it is the greater instance of ingratitude we can express towards our Lord and Master Jesus Christ.**

For if He came down from heaven, and shed His precious blood, to purchase these hearts of ours, and shall we only give Him half of them? Oh, how can we say we love Him, when our hearts are not wholly with Him? How can we call Him our Savior, when we will not endeavor sincerely to approve ourselves to Him, and so let Him see the travail of his soul, and be satisfied!

Had any of us purchased a slave at a most expensive rate, who was before involved in the utmost miseries and torments, and so must have continued for ever, had we shut up our heart of compassion from him; and were this slave afterwards to grow rebellious, and give us but half his service, how should we exclaim against his base ingratitude! And yet this base ungrateful slave you are, Oh man, who acknowledges yourself to be redeemed from infinite unavoidable misery and punishment by the death of Jesus Christ, and yet will not give yourself wholly to Him. But shall we deal with God our Maker in a manner we would not be dealt with by a man like ourselves? God forbid!

Let me add a word or two of exhortation to you, to excite you to be not only almost, but altogether Christians. Oh, let us scorn all base and treacherous treatment of our King and Savior, of our God and Creator. Let us not take some pains all our lives to go to heaven, and yet plunge ourselves into hell at last. Let us give to God our whole hearts, and no longer halt between two opinions. If the world be god, let us serve that; if pleasure be a god, let us serve that; but if the Lord be God, let us, oh let us, serve Him alone. Why, why should we stand out any longer? Why should we be so in love with slavery, as not wholly to renounce the world, the flesh, and the devil, which, like so many spiritual chains, bind down our souls, and hinder them from flying up to God? What are we afraid of? Is not God able to reward our entire obedience? If He is, as the almost Christian's lame way of serving Him seems to grant, why then will we not serve Him entirely? For the same reason we do so much, why do we not do more? Or do you think that being only half religious will make you happy, but that going farther will render you miserable and uneasy?

This, my brethren, is delusion all over; for what is it but this half piety, this wavering between God and the world, that makes so many that are seemingly well disposed, such utter strangers to the comforts of religion. They choose just so much of religion as will disturb them in their lusts, and follow their lusts so far as to deprive themselves of the comforts of religion. Whereas, on the contrary, would they sincerely leave all in affection, and give their hearts wholly to God, they would then (and they cannot until then) experience the unspeakable pleasure of having a mind at unity with itself, and enjoy such a peace of God, which even in this life passes all understanding, and which they were entire strangers to before.

It is true, if we will devote ourselves entirely to God, we must meet with contempt; but then it is because contempt is necessary to heal our pride. We must renounce some sensual pleasures; but then it is because those unfit us for spiritual ones, which are infinitely better. We must renounce the love of the world; but then it is that we may be filled with the love of God: and when that has once enlarged our hearts, we shall, like Jacob when he served for his beloved Rachel, think nothing too difficult to undergo, no hardships too tedious to endure, because of the love we shall then have for our dear Redeemer. Thus easy, thus delightful will be the ways of God even in this life. But when once we throw off these bodies, and our souls are filled with all the fullness of God, Oh what heart can conceive, what tongue can express, with what unspeakable joy and consolation shall we then look back on our past sincere and hearty services! Shall we then repent that we have done too much; or rather do you not think we shall be ashamed that we did no more; and blush that we were so backward to give up all to God when He intended hereafter to give us Himself?

Let me therefore, to conclude, exhort you my brethren, to have always before you the unspeakable happiness of enjoying God. And remember that every degree of holiness you neglect, every act of piety you omit, is a jewel taken out of your crown, a degree of blessedness lost in the vision of God. Oh, do but always think and act thus, and you will no longer be laboring to compound matters between God and the world; but, on the contrary, be daily endeavoring to give up yourselves more and more unto Him. You will be always watching, always praying, always aspiring after further degrees of purity and love, and consequently always preparing yourselves for a fuller sight and enjoyment of that God, in whose presence there is fullness of joy, and at whose right hand there are pleasures for evermore. Amen! ■

George Whitfield, 1714-1770, sparked and fanned the flame of the Great Awakening in America, and contributed untold riches to the state of the Church in America today. Hailed as possibly the greatest preacher that England ever produced, he was both a thoroughly engaging, impassioned orator and a dynamic, prolific and thought-provoking preacher. Transcripts of his sermons are available from a variety of sources, including anthologies and histories of the Great Awakening.

God's Ultimate Plan

by Rick Joyner

All Scripture references NAS unless otherwise indicated.

Repent therefore and return, that your sins may be wiped away, in order that times of refreshing may come from the presence of the Lord;

And that He may send Jesus, the Christ appointed for you,

Whom heaven must receive *until the period of restoration of all things* about which God spoke by the mouth of His holy prophets from ancient time (Acts 3:19-20).

The first two chapters in the Bible and then the last two make a complete story. Everything between those four chapters deals with one essential subject—restoring man and the creation to the place from which they have fallen. The process by which the Lord accomplishes this restoration is called redemption. Understanding redemption is fundamental to understanding all that God has done, is doing, or will do on the earth, from the fall until the earth is fully restored.

THE NEW CREATION

In the midst of God's great and epic plan to redeem His fallen creation, He determined to take what the enemy intended for evil and turn it into an even greater good. Those who participate with Him in His plan of redemption He has enabled to become a "new creation," which greatly transcends the original creation. We may think that there would be nothing more wonderful than to have the kind of relationship to God that Adam had before the fall, or that Moses had, who frequently talked with the Lord face to face. Who has not envied the disciples who walked with Jesus when He was on this earth? However, the Lord Jesus told His disciples that it was actually better for them if He departed this life so that the Holy Spirit could come to live in them. By this He stated that the gift of the Holy Spirit was actually to be esteemed above walking with Jesus when He was manifested as a man.

Through the new creation the gap between the spiritual and natural realms has been bridged. Men who are flesh can actually become partakers of the divine nature through Christ. Though we walk on the earth, we can be seated with Him in the heavenly places. In the original, uncorrupted creation God walked with man and had fellowship with him. In the new creation, God has come to live *in* man, calling us to be His eternal dwelling place. This is a much higher calling. Instead of death returning us to the dust, which was the curse upon the original creation, death is the gateway through which we enter heaven to live with Him eternally.

Every Christian has the power of the One who created the universe living within him. We also have the One who knows all things and controls all things living within us. The comprehension of this must be one of the greatest marvels from the angels in heaven to the demons in hell. Why would God so esteem men to choose us to be His temple? This may be even harder for us who are a part of the fallen race to understand, knowing our own corruption and tendency toward evil. Even so, once we who deserve it so little come to this understanding, we appreciate it even more. Those who are forgiven much will love much.

> IN THE NEW CREATION, GOD HAS COME TO LIVE IN MAN, CALLING US TO BE HIS ETERNAL DWELLING PLACE.

However, we cannot behold or become a part of this new creation without understanding, partaking of, and being a part of the implementation of the basic plan of redemption. The high calling of God to be a part of His new creation is a call to service. The higher the calling the more we are called to serve. Reconciling the world back to God is our basic ministry. Man turned from God but God never turned from man.

How many of us, if we knew that all of our best friends, who we had poured our whole life into for over three years, were going to desert us and even deny that they knew us, would still earnestly desire to have a last meal with them? After all that the Lord put into preparing the twelve, only one of them would be found at the base of the cross, standing with Him in His time of greatest need. Yet, the Lord never gave up on the others, and He never condemned them for failing Him so. The Bible is not a story about men who sought God, but about the way that God has sought men. Through all of the rebellion and rebuffs that men have given to Him, He has never given up on us. That is His nature, and it must also be ours if we are to be in unity with Him.

If we are going to be in unity with the Lord in His plan of redemption, we must learn to look past the failures of one another. Since the first century, the history of great men of God has far too often been that of great exploits only to be followed by a great fall at the end. The leaders of almost every great move of God have ended up persecuting the movements that followed them. There has hardly been an exception to this. The great men of Scripture often endured many failures, but ended in triumph. Since then it has too often been that leaders have many great successes, only to end in tragic defeat and delusion. One primary reason for this is probably found in the way we treat our fallen brethren. Rather than extending grace and mercy, the way that the Lord did, we often condemn them to a spiritual graveyard and have nothing else to do with them. Is this the example that the Lord left to us?

WHY HE IS RETURNING

When the Lord returns to "restore all things" He will come with a rod of iron to swiftly punish those who do not obey. However, this is obviously not the time when He has come to restore all things, because He has not yet returned. Sin is not swiftly punished, but rather rewarded. Satan is the ruler of this present evil age and he does reward those who bow down to him, that is, who will live according to his ways. This is the age and the environment when the Lord is choosing those who will be a part of His "new creation," who will be members of His own household and reign with Him. This is the highest calling in the creation and their worship and obedience must be proven. Adam lived in a perfect world but still chose to disobey. Those of the new creation will have lived in a dark and evil world that rewards sin, but will have chosen to obey against all of the pressures and influences of this evil age.

Jesus was "the last Adam" (see I Corinthians 15:45). As Adam began the first race of men, Jesus also began a new race, a spiritual one. This new race transforms men from the first creation into a new race that is far greater than the first. However, the purpose of the new creation is the redemption of the first creation. We must never forget that the Lord fully intends to "restore all things," which is the reason for His return. If He did not intend to restore the earth He would have just snatched us away to heaven and then destroyed the earth. He is coming back, and bringing us with Him, to rule over it until the restoration is complete.

When Jesus saw what was wrong with the world, He did not condemn it—it was already condemned; He laid down His life for it. It is likewise the nature of those who are united to Him to lay down their lives to help restore those who are the slaves of this evil age. He knows that we will not be fully successful until He returns. One reason that He did not just snatch us away to heaven as soon as we committed our lives to follow Him was for our sake—to learn and to prove our devotion to Him and His purposes.

THE BOB JONES SAGA

When the chronicles of heaven are read on that great Judgment Day, I am convinced that Bob Jones, a prophet from Independence, Missouri, will be honored as one who helped greatly to prepare the last day ministry of the church. From one end of the earth to the other I have met people who claim that a word from Bob Jones changed their life, or set them on the course to the ministry they are now in. But like the apostle

Peter, Bob's life has been a course of extraordinary spiritual accomplishments, followed by humiliating mistakes. Both his accomplishments and his mistakes are important for us to understand if we are to be prepared for what is coming.

Right after the Lord said to Peter, **"Blessed are you, Simon Barjona, because flesh and blood did not reveal this to you, but My Father who is in heaven" (Matthew 16:17),** the Lord gave him the keys of the kingdom of heaven. Then the very next thing that He said to Peter was, **"Get behind Me, Satan!" (verse 23).** Right after Peter received a word straight from the Father, he received one straight from the enemy. Even though Peter would fall hard at times, he would get up and keep going. Therefore, even after his mistakes, the Lord did not take the keys to the kingdom away from him. In spite of his flaws, Peter, who would get out of the boat to walk on water, was the disciple most likely to use the keys to open the doors.

With Bob Jones we have a similar dilemma. You cannot be around Bob very long without realizing that he is receiving revelation straight from the Father. Like Peter, he has also succumbed to some of the enemy's most destructive traps. Even so, Bob keeps getting back up, dusts himself off, and like the "Energizer Bunny," he keeps going, and going, and going.

A KEY TO THE KINGDOM

Bob obviously does have some of the keys to the kingdom. He walks in a spiritual realm that is in many ways unlike anyone I have ever met. It is real and it is God. However, Bob does not just have some of the keys to the kingdom—he represents one of them. He will be either a stepping stone or stumbling block to the kind of prophetic authority that we must have to accomplish our mission in the last days.

God does not tempt us, but He does test us. His tests are given for the purpose of qualifying us for promotions to the next grade, to give us more spiritual authority. Bob Jones is a test that many of us will have to pass before we can go on. Others may not have to pass the test with Bob Jones, but they will be given similar vessels, or situations, that they will have to learn to properly deal with before they, too, can go further.

Is this biblical? Yes. This is the same kind of test that the Galatians had to pass to receive Paul (see Galatians 4:13-14). This is not to imply that Bob Jones is on the level of Paul the apostle, but the Lord often makes His vessels a test that will separate those who really love the truth from those who judge by appearances. Jonah was also such a vessel, as were many of the other prophets in Scripture. We now esteem Isaiah, but how many of us would have identified ourselves with a prophet who went around naked for three and a half years? How many of us would have asked John the Baptist over for Sunday dinner? Would you have wanted to live next door to Hosea and his harlot wife? How many of us, had we been those with great religious influence, would really have been open to listen to a carpenter from Nazareth? In fact, almost all of God's vessels will be a major test for the flesh, and those who trust in the arm of the flesh will not pass this test.

HIGHLIGHTS

Bob Jones' prophetic revelation is the most extraordinary I have ever witnessed. His prophetic gifts are of true biblical stature. A number of times Bob has told me the names of people that I was going to meet, and many other details about them. He has told me details about meetings which I was going to attend months, and in one case, years before they were even scheduled. He has called me to tell me the dream or vision that I had, and then interpreted it. He prophesied the birth of our third child two years before, including the day she would be born and her weight, accurately. Twice he has told me of visitations from the Lord that I was to receive, and the commission that was coming with it, along with the time and place that it would happen. I have heard him prophesy a number of national and international events, and natural disasters, with astonishing detail and accuracy. I have not personally witnessed the authority over demons, or the gifts of healings and miracles, following any other person like they do Bob. This is not to say that they don't, but I have not witnessed it.

Even more important than the signs that follow his life is that when Bob comes to a church or city almost every person he encounters is left functioning on a higher spiritual level. He stirs up the gifts in others. He does it in such a way that imparts faith in God, not just His gifts. He will patiently spend hours a day ministering to individuals, not distinguishing between the high and the lowly, the famous or the infamous. The love of God so exudes from him that he makes everyone feel like the most important person in the world. Children adore him like he does them. He can spend a few minutes with a child and impart such a zeal for God that it can carry them for years above the turbulence of youth.

THE LOWLIGHTS

Like many prophetic people, Bob has been deeply wounded by rejection and misunderstanding. At times he has allowed the rejection to turn into bitterness, and bitterness will always defile. Bitterness is spiritual madness. For a time Bob allowed bitterness to drive him to what he himself called "spiritual insanity." The greater the anointing and spiritual authority that one walks in, the greater the potential fall and deception that they can suffer if they give themselves over to sin. Bob fell to some of the lowest levels of deception and sin. To his credit, he asked me to tell the whole story without holding anything back, knowing that it could further hurt his ministry or reputation, but being even more concerned that it could help save others from falling to the same traps.

In the late 1980s, Bob Jones and the Kansas City Fellowship came under one of the most ruthless attacks of the accuser I have ever witnessed. As is the case with most "attackers," their accuser was hiding serious sin in his own life. Bob knew it, and other prophetic people knew. Even so, the leaders of KCF (now Metro Vineyard Fellowship), determined to use this trial to humble themselves before God to seek more of His grace. They did not defend themselves against the slander and false accusations, but rather searched the accusations for any degree of truth so that they could publicly repent of them.

When years later the sins of their accuser were publicly revealed, the Metro Vineyard church did not gloat, but the leaders and the people wept in sincere remorse at the fall of a brother, knowing that many more Christians would be wounded. After hearing this I heard one man remark, "There really are some true Christians in the church!"

In the heat of the attack, Bob was disciplined for some of the mistakes that he had made, and his tendency to be too loose in both sharing and applying sensitive prophetic information. Bob accepted this relatively well until he felt that no one had properly defended him against the false accusations and slander. His rejection turned to bitterness and resentment. Defilement soon followed. Bob then began to rationalize that if his accuser could get away with adultery, with seemingly no repercussions, he could mess around a little and get away

> *If we cannot restore our fallen brothers and sisters, how can we preach redemption, reconciliation and forgiveness to the world.*

with it. Darkness then overtook him like a flood. He even used his extraordinary prophetic gifts to manipulate a mother and daughter that he was counseling. Serious sexual misconduct followed. Though it stopped short of adultery, in Bob's own words, what was done was no

less serious, and a woman and her daughter had been deeply wounded.

THE DELUSIONS OF POWER

Months before his fall Bob had called me asking for help. He had prayed for a spirit of lust to be broken off of a well-known evangelist, but he had done this without permission from the Lord. In Bob's words, when he did this it "jumped on" him, and he could not shake it. I had witnessed Bob cast out many powerful demons that others could not handle. I just could not imagine any demon staying around him for very long, so I brushed off his request for help. Several times over the next few months Bob called me for help, and each time I tried to encourage him that no demon could stay close to him long. The next time I saw Bob I was shocked by the power of the spirit I saw oppressing him. I did not want to make the same mistake that he had by trying to take authority over something that powerful alone, so I found Mahesh Chavda, and we prayed together for it to be broken off of him. It departed and Bob changed before our eyes.

When it later surfaced just how far Bob had fallen into sexual misconduct, I was grieved over how I had let him down when he had cried out for help. I had been overly awed by Bob's gifts and spiritual authority over demons. Since then I have come to understand that the greater the anointing, the greater the blind spots can also be. Even the greatest man of God is fallible, and if we ever think that we cannot fall we have probably already begun to.

I was not the only one to make a mistake with Bob during this time, or after it. There have been reactions and over-reactions, but in those trying times I was surprised that the situation was handled as well as it was. Even so, a number of us were shown last December that until the situation with Bob Jones was properly resolved, which includes his full restoration to his proper place in the church, we ourselves would go no further. In many ways, the lessons learned from this whole situation are essential for us to understand before the Lord can endorse us with any more anointing or authority.

What Bob did was inexcusable, and he cannot shift the blame to anyone else for his own sins. God does not forgive excuses; He forgives sins. In Bob's own words he fell into the depths of spiritual delusion and carnal corruption. He does not want to hide it, but rather wants to use it as an example to help prevent others from making the same mistakes. This is both very noble, and very important. One reason why the Lord has placed Bob as a test to many is that he represents the condition of not only many prophetic people, but to some degree, the church as a whole. By learning how to heal, restore, and protect Bob we will learn what it will take to heal, restore, and protect multitudes who have fallen to different aspects of the same problems.

GOD'S PRIMARY BUSINESS

After King David fell into sin with Bathsheba, Scripture says that all of Israel went astray and followed after Absalom. For the people of Israel it was probably very hard for them to believe that someone who had fallen into such debauchery could still be anointed. However, the Lord was not surprised by what happened. He knew what was in David's heart when He called him. He knew that it was going to happen when He made him the king. He used David before the fall, and after it.

Our God is in the redemption business. That is His primary work on this earth at this time. Yet we who have been the recipients of His great grace often have the most difficulty in extending it to others. We must get this right if we are going to properly represent Him on this earth.

THE HIGHEST CALLING

When all of Israel went astray and followed after Absalom, Zadok, the high priest, picked up the ark and followed David. He followed him at the risk of not only his ministry, but his life. Even if they were to survive, it appeared very unlikely that David would be restored to the throne. At best, those who followed him would probably spend the rest of their lives living in caves and holes in the ground, as they had when being pursued by King Saul. Even so, Zadok was more faithful to the anointing than he was to political expediency, or even his own welfare. He knew that, regardless of David's great sin, the anointing was still on him. Zadok simply followed God regardless of the cost.

God rewarded Zadok's courage and faithfulness with one of the greatest blessings recorded in the Scriptures. He was promised that his sons would minister to the Lord personally (see Ezekiel 40:46 and 44:15-16), essentially saying that they would be the closest to the Lord. When the Jews declared to Jesus that they were the sons of Abraham, He replied that if they were the sons of Abraham they would do the deeds of Abraham. Likewise, those who are the true sons of Zadok are those who do the deeds of Zadok. The true sons of Zadok are those who will follow the anointing regardless of the risk. They are the ones who will be the closest to the Lord and serve Him personally.

As Paul Cain declared in one of his most prophetic messages of the last few years, we will all have to choose between the anointing and respectability. Passing the test—that we can rise above spiritual politics to be faithful to what is right—is one of the most important tests that anyone called to walk in spiritual authority must pass. Will we, like King Saul, make our decisions based on the pressures of the people or the political consequences? Or will we, like King David, rise above the pressures of the people and the circumstances of this world, to always seek the Lord's will first? A great demarcation always comes to the leadership of the church based on this one issue.

Those who are not directly confronted with the Bob Jones test will be confronted by similar people or circumstances that will test their hearts on this same issue. Ultimately, every individual, church, movement and many cities will

have to pass this test before they will be endorsed with the anointing that will be required by those who will be a part of the last day ministry of the church.

RESTORATION IS NOT OPTIONAL

Galatians 6:1 (NKJV) states, **"If a man is overtaken in *ANY TRESPASS*, you who are spiritual *restore* such a one in a spirit of gentleness, considering yourself lest you also be tempted."** Regardless of how personally distasteful someone's sin may be to us, we are not given the choice as to whether we will restore them or not, or we ourselves will be in jeopardy of falling to the same temptations. There is not a single one of us who stands to any degree except for the grace of God. If we cannot restore our fallen brothers and sisters, how can we preach redemption, reconciliation and forgiveness to the world?

After his fall, King David rose to much greater heights of spiritual authority and prophetic revelation. So has Bob Jones. So can Jim Bakker, Jimmy Swaggart and many others who have been tripped up by the enemy, or have been carried away with their own lusts. It is just as possible for the accuser who rose up against Bob and the Kansas City Fellowship to be restored and rise to an even greater level of spiritual authority. The Lord loves everyone of them. If we are in unity with Him should we not be desiring and seeking this for our fallen brothers?

Renewal in the Body of Christ would best not be seen as a new movement in the church but as the Church in movement. **Unknown**

Those who are forgiven much, love much. God loves all men and sincerely desires for all to be saved. All that the enemy meant for evil the Lord intends to use as testimonies of His power of redemption. Strangely, Christians seem to now have more trouble forgiving each other than the heathen do. We must believe in the Lord's power of redemption before the world is going to believe us. These men, and the multitude of others who have fallen to various traps of the enemy, even "any trespass," must be restored, or we will continue to be subject to the same temptations.

> IT IS ONLY THROUGH THE PROCESS OF RESTORATION THAT WE WILL LEARN WHERE THE GATES OF HELL ARE, AND HOW TO SHUT THEM.

Restoring is more than just forgiving. We can apologize to these fallen brothers or sisters to appease our consciences, but that is not enough to pass the test. *They must be restored.* This does not imply in any way that the biblical standards of integrity should be compromised, or that a process that insures restoration should not be implemented. Even so, we must do whatever it takes for the fallen to be fully restored. Our Father does not want any of His children left in the ditch by their brothers and sisters. That is not the only reason why we are required to restore those who have fallen. It is only through the process of restoration that we will learn where the gates of hell are, and how to shut them. The gates of hell are the places that the enemy is using to gain access into the world, the church, and our own lives.

THE REWARD

At our spring conference, I publicly acknowledged the failures in my relationship to Bob Jones. I also brought him to the platform to briefly share what was on his heart in order to publicly acknowledge that I receive Bob and his ministry. However, I can only do this for myself and the ministry that I have been made a steward over. I did at the time what I felt I needed to do to make things right with my brother, and to be obedient to the Lord. I am thankful that the Lord confirmed it afterwards in a way that would make it hard for me to now doubt it. Even so, as Francis Frangipane likes to say, "We seldom pass God's tests with a perfect score." I do not presume that I am doing everything perfectly, or maybe even very well, but even the fumbling steps that we made have resulted in an unprecedented grace being released on us. When a few friends and I invited Bob Jones to Moravian Falls to view a fulfillment to one of his own prophecies, and we had a time of reconciliation and acknowledging his ministry to us, the heavens opened and we experienced the grace and presence of God in many ways which transcends anything I have ever experienced before. When we brought Bob to the conference and acknowledged his place with us, the conference went to a level that we have not experienced before.

At each of our conferences the Lord has given me more encouragement about the spiritual condition of the people attending. One of the greatest encouragements yet was the response of the people to Bob, who gave him the longest standing ovation that I think I have ever seen. If we receive a prophet in the name of a prophet we will receive a prophet's reward. If we receive a prophet as anything less, we will receive that much less. The whole church is about to be in an increasingly desperate need of the prophetic ministry. To get there we are going to have to accept many, and very possibly most, people in a condition that is less than most of us would desire. They will need healing and restoration. It will not be easy, but the reward will be worth it.

At MorningStar we have been blessed beyond our dreams by the quality of prophetic ministries that we have been sent, and that are being raised up in our midst. The rewards of this have been far beyond our expectations. For some reason, when we received Bob Jones, the rewards seemed to multiply. Since then, not only our meetings, but our daily lives have been filled with awe and wonder at the great things the Lord is doing. The prophetic people here almost uniformly go to a new level of hearing from God whenever Bob comes to town. Dreams, visions and visitations increase dramatically. But even more wonderful than all of that, the manifest presence of the Lord increases. Instead of just going from meeting to meeting, we are going from encounter to encounter with the Son of God. The love for Jesus is growing in His people here. I have never experienced the kind of worship that we have been having lately, and it is because of the genuine love for the Lord that is growing in His people.

THE PRICE

This kind of outpouring does not come with any man, including Bob Jones. It does come with the prophetic ministry. All of the ministries are an aspect of the Lord's own ministry and Person in our midst. As we receive them we receive Him. The prophetic ministry is used to testify of the heart and mind of God in our present circumstances, which makes us more aware of the "presence" of the Lord. That is why Paul exhorted the Corinthians to, **"Desire earnestly spiritual gifts, but** *especially that you may prophesy*** (I Corinthians 14:1).** Miracles will draw you to the hand of God, but true prophecy will draw you to His face. **"The testimony of Jesus is the spirit of prophecy" (Revelation 19:10).**

Even so, prophecy has usually come in the most unseemly packages, just as the Lord Himself came in a form that would separate those who loved the anointing more than they loved respectability. Respectability with men is almost always the price that we must pay for the anointing, and those who love the approval of men will not pay it.

There is also another price that must be paid if we want the reward of a true prophetic ministry—troubles, tribulations and persecution. Satan knows very well that when the bride is ready, his time is short. The prophetic ministry has an important role to play in preparing a pure and spotless bride fit for the King. That is why the Lord gives specific warnings about doing His prophets harm.

This is not out of favoritism for the prophets, but because He knows that the enemy will always try to incite people to harm the prophets. Just as John the Baptist had to be sent to prepare the way for the Lord the first time He came, the prophetic ministry is essential for preparing for His return, and for preparing His bride. The enemy seems to know this even better than the church, and will release a massive onslaught against the prophetic everywhere it arises.

The prophetic ministry will also be a threat to those who have established their authority or influence over the people through counterfeit spiritual authority, or who have sin in their life. The prophetic ministry will expose sin, and as we should have learned well over the last decade, those who are hiding sin will often become attackers. The prophetic, which does have the power to expose things that may have otherwise remained hidden, will usually be the target of these attacks. Psychologists call this presenting a bold exterior to hide corruption on the inside. Jesus called them "whitewashed graves" that looked good on the outside but were full of death inside. You will almost always find that those who most viciously attack others are those who likewise have the most to hide.

A TEST WITH TWO SIDES

These attacks are allowed by God as a test for the prophetic. By his own admission, Bob failed this test badly. First he took the wounds and turned inward with rejection. Then he turned outward and became bitter, often railing and accusing his friends that he felt had let him down, or authorities who had to discipline him. The test of the prophetic goes both ways.

They must also pass the test that they have become to others. Many prophetic people will fail this test, but that does not mean that they are finished. As Francis also once said, "You don't really fail God's tests, you just keep taking them until you pass."

THE UNHOLY WAR

Presently there is a war going on between the pastoral and prophetic ministries. Pastors are claiming that the prophets have almost killed their ministries, and prophets are claiming that pastors are always trying to destroy their ministries. As is usually the case, there is truth to both sides. However, neither will come into their rightful place, or be able to bring the church into her place, without each other, along with all of the ministries given for the equipping of the church.

As the Lord told Bobby Conner, one reason that the general anointing level is so low in the church is that the Lord had to take the swords out of our hands because we were using them on each other more than on the enemy. In general, we are in a time like that of King Saul, when the Lord allowed the Philistines to take all of the weapons away from Israel, and even required the Israelites to pay the Philistines to sharpen their farming tools. Until an authority with the nature of David arises, He cannot trust His people with the divinely powerful weapons because we are more prone to use them on each other than on the enemy.

Bob Jones, like the prophetic ministry in general, and much like the church in general, has some extraordinary gifts. He also has some deep, unhealed wounds that must be healed. Bob has been a faithful friend, and one of the greatest helps to me, my family, and my ministry. I would want to see him fully restored if for no other reason than that, but I have far greater reasons. I believe that he also represents in an important way what it will take to see a true prophetic ministry released to the church, and a church that walks in true spiritual authority released to the world.

I have been warned by good friends that Bob has the potential to cause great embarrassment and harm to my ministry. I have never been ignorant of that possibility. I know, and he knows, that he still has rejection and some bitterness in his life. Though he is making progress and overcoming it, as long as it remains, there is great potential for another fall. I sincerely appreciate the concern of my friends, but I am trying very hard not to be concerned about either my reputation or my ministry, but simply doing the will of God. My standing before the Judge will not be based on how many books I distribute. The true food of every true ministry is to do the will of the One who has sent him.

It is part of my calling to help restore the prophetic ministry to the church. I know that I am but one of many, and do not in any way consider myself to be the most important. I simply want to be faithful to my calling. That requires me to be faithful to Bob for as long as he at least tries to be faithful to God. It requires me to welcome many others who are wounded, rejected and bitter. It requires me to take all of the persecution and accusation that constantly follows those who are now trying to walk in a prophetic calling. I personally am very glad to do it, and think that the rewards of helping this ministry far outweigh the problems.

FAIRNESS OR GRACE?

Bob became discouraged because he did not see his accuser, who was hiding serious sin in his own life, exposed. The Lord intended to expose the accuser, but not until He had finished the work that He wanted to do in Bob. God's timing often offends our own sense of justice or fairness. This was Jonah's problem. He did not want to look like a false prophet. But almost every true prophet looked like a false prophet in his own time. It was the false prophets who were much more prone to be generally accepted.

God's purpose is not bound up in our reputation, and we should all be thankful that He is not trying to be just or fair, but rather merciful. To be truly prophetic requires that, if we know that we are known by God and sent by Him, it really must not matter what anyone else thinks of us. If we are going to be a prophetic people, and help restore a prophetic church, we must have the constitution of Elijah, who could even stand before the king and say, **"As the LORD, the God of Israel lives, *before whom I stand . . .*" (I Kings 17:1).** By this Elijah was saying, "I am not standing in front of you, Ahab. You're just a man. I stand before the living God. I live my life before God, not men." Until we have this attitude, we will not be free to either love men properly, or speak the truth to them without compromise, both of which are required of true prophetic ministry. ∎

Harry went to church

and listened to the message, which challenged him to be more evangelistic. The pastor asked whether those attending had actively worked to bring their colleagues and neighbors to the Lord. Harry thought about it, and realized that he had actually done very little in that area. He went to another meeting that week in which the message was about tithing, and realized that he was not giving enough money. He wanted to give more, but he had been so busy that he had not found the time to think through the family budget and decide what he should do about it. Then he wondered how he would decide between the multitude of requests for support that he had received in the past month.

His tape of the month from a ministry arrived, and he was called to spend more time in prayer and intercession. He picked up a book, and read about how he needed to spend more time with his children, including reading their school books so that he would be aware of what they were being taught. A pamphlet then arrived in the mail asking him to join an anti-abortion march. Another told about the forthcoming March for Jesus to take place in the same weekend. His wife left her Bible open to the Scripture that read, "Husbands, love your wives . . ."

His work was becoming more and more demanding. His company had been working on re-engineering, which meant that his job now included more responsibility than previously. He was aware that the Bible calls us to do our work as unto the Lord, so was trying his best to keep up with the new demands. One night, Harry fell before the Lord, and cried out to Him, "Lord, you said that your burden is light. Either You did not mean what you said, or I am missing something. This burden is so heavy that I am being crushed even thinking about it."

Harry's dilemma is not uncommon in the Christian world today. We know that there is so much to be done, but the harder we try, the more we see we are failing. There are several common responses to this:

The first is to stop trying. Once we realize that no matter how hard we try, we cannot make a dent in what needs to be done, motivation is easily lost. This is the plight of much of the church: we refuse to hear anymore when we are being called to greater endeavors. To protect ourselves, we let the words wash over us. The frustrated pastors complain that the whole congregation just sits there while the pastor carries the whole burden with very little assistance.

Another response is to fall into legalism and imbalance. We choose one area where we are determined to succeed. We close our minds to other areas. This does not promote balanced spiritual growth, and will usually isolate us from those who have chosen other areas in which to excel.

The third response is to swing wildly from challenge to challenge until we become so exhausted that we finally submit to defeat and join those in the first category, collapsing into our pew.

Could all of this be a reason for the Laodicean lukewarmness that now prevails over so much of the Western church? It seems that most of the demands for increased activity and productivity are now becoming counter-productive, turning more people off than on. What can we do to bring this back into a proper balance?

Lessons from Physical Fitness

The following is a true story. Megan (not her real name) was 55 years old. She had smoked for 40 years. She stopped smoking, and for two years ate to compensate for it. By age 57, she had become 30 pounds overweight. Her lifestyle had always been sedentary. Periodically, Megan would decide that she needed to do something about the situation. She would go on a crash diet while simultaneously beginning an intensive program of exercise. The diet would last a couple of days at the longest. The exercise lasted until she became exhausted (which was not long) or until she got injured. It was never more than one week until she was back where she had started.

One day, Megan accepted the fact that the situation could not be rectified overnight. She began to exercise gently but consistently. A personal trainer worked with her periodically to show her how much weight to add on days when she did strength training, how to vary her exercise, and to check her form. Often, the trainer counseled her to cut back on her exercise, reminding Megan that there was more danger from burnout and injury than from exercising at a slightly lower level of intensity than what might be optimal.

The trainer also counseled Megan on her diet. It was difficult for Megan to get used to bread without butter, vegetables rather than chips, and oatmeal for breakfast rather than donuts, but over time she made the transition. Previously she had failed when she became too hungry, but now she never reached that level of hunger because she ate plenty, but differently. At the end of six months, Megan had gone from 33% fat to 22%, by the end of one year she was at 17% fat (ideal for women). She continued to gain strength and endurance. As her 60th birthday approached, she took great

by Suzanne de Treville

enjoyment from the fact that she was stronger and healthier than she had been in her 30s.

Applying the Lessons

How does this example apply to our spiritual growth? Many of us resemble Megan in our spiritual lives. We are fat, sedentary and weak. When we see our condition, we frantically attempt to change it, but we are defeated because we try to do too much too fast. Just as Megan had to put herself into the hands of a trainer who could counsel her, so we need to put ourselves into our Lord's hands, trusting Him to bring us to spiritual fitness in His time.

What can we expect Him to do? He will give us a daily exercise program! When Megan started the program that her trainer gave her, she usually felt that the exercises were too easy. She had grown up in the "no pain, no gain" era, and thought that the exercise would not help unless she was really suffering. So it is when our "Trainer" gives us our assignment. We want to go off to Africa for missions, while He asks us to babysit with our neighbor's kids so they can go to a prayer meeting. Each day, we get our assignments. Each day, as we complete these assignments alone we get stronger, and the work of the Body gets done.

Special Training

Consider it pure joy, my brothers, whenever you face trials of many kinds,

because you know that the testing of your faith develops perseverance.

Perseverance must finish its work so that you may be mature and complete, not lacking anything (James 1:2-4).

The Lord's spiritual fitness training always includes some trials. Every trial is for the purpose of helping us grow spiritually. Therefore, if we are wise we will seize every trial as an opportunity from God for our benefit. Like final exams in school, God's tests are for the purpose of promoting us to new levels. However, we often miss some of the most important ones because they are too small. The big ones are easy to see, but most of us will endure some type of small test each day. If we would discern them and use them properly, we would probably advance much further and quicker than we would because of the occasional greater trials. Remember, it is "the little foxes that spoil the vine," and it can be the little trials that help us to preserve it. Jesus is the Vine and preserving the vine is to maintain our connection to Him.

I recently had a day when nothing went right. Everything I picked up I dropped. Every task I tried to complete had to be done two or three times. I felt as though I were going through the day in slow motion, as the pile of work to be done got higher by the minute. I went before the Lord to explain to Him that something fundamental was wrong. He answered me that He had organized some "endurance training" for me in allowing my normal tasks to be much more difficult. He explained to me first that this would not last forever. Just as aerobics classes stop after an hour, He promised that this would go for a short time, then things would revert to normal. Isaiah 28:28 (NAS) says, **"Grain for bread is crushed, indeed, he does not continue to thresh it forever. Because the wheel of his cart and his horses eventually damage it, he does not thresh it longer."** The Lord will not allow us to be "crushed" beyond what is necessary to make us into the bread that He is seeking to serve His church.

Second, the Lord promised that if I would continue putting one foot in front of the other, even though I felt like I was getting nothing done despite working as hard as I could, that evening I would be surprised by how much I had gotten done. He also promised that this training would make me stronger very quickly. He reminded me of how I have enjoyed the extra endurance that has come from my physical endurance training, and that I would likewise appreciate the spiritual fruit of this exercise.

During this time I had an important business trip in which I would be facing many difficulties. I was amazed at how the Lord went before me and gave me such grace and favor that much more was accomplished than I had dreamed possible. The Lord assured me that this grace had been gained by submitting to the previous smaller trials.

I sat at the airport on the way home, reading a wonderful Christian book, rejoicing in my spirit in the incredible goodness of the Lord. Then I checked my ticket, and noticed that it said economy class. I had paid for business class and was looking forward to flying home in the extra comfort, but they had accidentally put me in economy. I immediately shut down my praise session, closed my book, and stood up to go tell SwissAir that they needed to get me into the business class section! As I stood, the Lord spoke to my heart and asked me, "Can you receive this as being from My hand?" I finally agreed, grudgingly, to fly home economy class trusting that it was from the Lord's hand for my best. I did not understand, but figured that it was better to make a mistake in the direction of obedience than to insist on my rights. After I obeyed, He began to show me His gift.

He says, **"Humble yourselves before the Lord, and he will lift you up" (James 4:10).** He allowed me to humble myself before Him in thanksgiving for His remarkable blessings through accepting the economy class flight. This then protected me from the sin that so easily accompanies a great victory —pride! The next few days were full of small and precious gifts from the Lord to me just letting me know that He had been pleased by my obedience. What a small thing it was to take that economy class seat, what a hard struggle it entailed, and how great the results from that one "training session."

> Every trial is for the purpose of helping us grow **spiritually.**

Because the assignments produce fast results we can look at our progress and see that we have gotten stronger month to month. This encourages us to greater obedience. At the same time, we see the wisdom of the Trainer in cutting back certain assignments during times of pressure, and we begin to trust Him that He will not crush us beneath the weight of a program that is too hard for us. We begin to see that we can submit ourselves to His discipline for the rest of our lives, continually in strength.

When Megan began her exercise regimen, the amount of weight that she was able to lift was pitiful. So it is with us when the Lord begins to train us. We run out to the spiritual weight room, and immediately pile on the same weights that we see the spiritual giants next to us piling on. They intercede for eight hours at a time, so we try it, too—once! Our Master gives us the assignment of sitting before Him for five minutes, and we feel that it is pitiful. However, those of us who embrace this pitiful weight and lift it faithfully grow in strength more rapidly than anyone would ever expect. Now, when Megan goes into the weight room, many young men are amazed at her lifting capacity! So it will be with us.

Types of Spiritual Fitness Training

While this list is far from comprehensive, it is useful to consider some of the areas where we can expect the Lord to be sending us fitness exercises:

1. Faith. He begins by challenging our faith in small ways. One that He often uses in my life is simply believing that He will get me to an appointment on time. How does it work in practice? I am sitting in the car on the way to a class that I am to teach. I am typically running late. I first review whether I have been rebellious or disobedient in getting ready: if so, I repent. Most of the time these days, however, the cause of the lateness has not been my own sin but my exercise time! I sit in the car practicing resting in the knowledge that He is in control and in charge of every detail. After two years of this training, my faith in His care of little things is much stronger and I constantly witness His provision here.

Then He moves me on to bigger challenges. I sat in an important business meeting in a foreign country having just realized that my passport was lost. My schedule did not allow any time for delays (like having a new passport issued). My flesh wanted to leave the meeting, but in my spirit I realized that this was probably a more advanced faith exercise. I committed both passport and schedule into the Lord's care. I had to choose between trusting that He was in control, which meant that I could complete my work, or I could believe that it was up to me to find the passport, in which case I should leave the meeting and go into action. I told Him that I would take the decision to trust Him and rest, and that if I was wrong and needed to go into action would He please show me? I sat in that meeting and disciplined myself to concentrate. My flesh did not want to obey; it was as hard as the most difficult weight training I have ever done. At the end of the meeting, the secretary came and told me that my passport was found.

As we learn to expect the Lord to provide this kind of opportunity, we see events in our lives in a whole new way. This faith muscle gets built up fast—and we will need it to be strong enough in faith to accomplish our work as the harvest picks up speed.

2. Waiting. We as people hate to wait. I personally would rather spend an hour digging ditches than waiting for someone. This, unfortunately, is inconsistent with the Lord's desire, and His usual training for us. Waiting produces endurance in our faith.

He gave me a picture of Him getting the church ready for His coming as being like a parent trying to leave for a wonderful party with a group of small children. What the parent really needs is for the children to stay in the entryway keeping their clothes clean, not fighting with each other, and available and listening to the parent's voice. As His coming approaches, we understand better and better that the ability to wait for Him is at least as important as our activity. He knows, however, that especially in these times, waiting is not our strongest point. He provides exercises that over time increase our ability to wait: traffic lights, children, a package that we are expecting that does not show up. Waiting is not easy, but it is essential spiritual training.

3. Turning to Him in times of stress. He wants us to have as an instant reflex that we turn to Him when under pressure rather than reacting in our flesh. Nothing happens to us by coincident, and I have been learning that I can receive everything that happens as being from His hand. Even if it is the devil who is behind a thing, the Lord has allowed it for a reason. If we would learn to always turn to Him first when a trial comes upon us, our lives would probably be significantly easier and more fruitful than they now are.

4. Knowing that His strength is made perfect in weakness. I am personally devoted to physical fitness. The norm in my life has been to walk in exceptional physical strength and blessing, but the Lord reserves the right to allow me to suffer problems that cast me even more upon His strength and provision. Christians, regardless of their theology, do suffer physical illness and other afflictions. Even though the Lord may not cause them, He obviously allows these trials *for our good.* Overcoming does not consist in denying the problem, but in finding His strength in the midst of it.

5. Stretching. As soon as a muscle is strengthened, it must be stretched, and the same is true in the spirit. There are many times in the day when I realize that the Lord is stretching me, and it tends to be painful. Now that I have learned that it is stretching, I can submit to it as I do to physical stretching—by relaxing and submitting to the stretch, much of the pain is alleviated. Whenever we are being stretched in spirit we must not allow this to rob us of the rest that we have in Christ.

Our Spiritual Diet as We Build Fitness

Now let's go to the area that many of us will find more difficult: the area of food. It was tough for Megan to switch from fatty junk food (which she loved) to low fat, nourishing food. So we shrink from the idea of giving up our fatty, spiritual junk food in favor of what is better for us. What are some examples of spiritual junk food? Television and many popular novels could head the list. Reading the Bible and Christian classics seem like a poor substitute, but once we have made the transition, we will enjoy them more than we did the spiritual junk food, and we will feel much better too.

Another example of spiritual junk food is gossip and idle conversation. Some of this might even be classified as a poison more than just junk food. What a pleasure it is to sometimes spend a couple of hours on the telephone talking about others in a way that really is not edifying. However, this pleasure can be very costly to us and the body of Christ. This is the same kind of pleasure we may receive from eating a donut, or pastry. It tastes good while we are doing it, but its long term effect can be very bad. Ephesians 4:29 (NAS) says, **"Let no unwholesome word proceed from your mouth, but only such a word as is good for edification according to the need of the moment, that it may give grace to those who hear."**

Meeting for prayer, worship, or solid teaching may seem boring. However, if we would discipline ourselves to only partake of that which is good for us we would feel much better than most of us do now, not to mention be much more pleasing to the Lord. Often what may at first not taste as good, will later taste better, and result in a much happier and more fruitful life.

When Megan's trainer told her which foods would build health and support her growing in strength, and which would hinder, Megan had a hard time with it. She turned to the Lord, and asked Him to help her make good choices. He answered that prayer, and gave her grace on a moment by moment basis to eat what was right. Over time it became much easier for her, but at the beginning she needed constant grace. So it is as we shift to nourishing spiritual food. The Lord knows our hearts, and is not offended if we go to Him, praying, "Lord, I am hungry for television, movies, useless books and other spiritual food that does not give me what I need."

We know from James 4:6 (NKJV) that **"God resists the proud, but gives grace to the humble."** A number of times in Scripture we see that the people of God "humbled themselves with fasting." Periodic fasting from physical food has obvious physical and spiritual benefits, but so can fasting from other things. If we were to fast from television for a week, and use that time for reading quality Christian books, listening to tapes, and reading our Bibles, the immediate and long term benefit would probably spoil us into continuing until we no longer had any desire for television. The increased richness of our lives, as well as the removal of the guilt, and the evil that we often allow our minds to be bombarded with, can result in a huge change in the quality of our life.

Too Much of a Good Thing

As Megan progressed in her fitness development, she had a rude shock. She was only eating healthy food, but she again started to gain a few pounds! She was horrified, and complained to her trainer. The trainer was sympathetic, but told her some bad news: it is possible to eat too much good food!

The same applies to us spiritually. If we eat too much good food without "working it off," we will grow fat spiritually. In my early Christian walk, I devoured books, often reading more than a book a day. I also listened to many tapes, and would move heaven and earth to get to a meeting where there would be a good speaker. Now, the Lord holds me back, often allowing me to read only a few pages of a book rather than the whole thing. He has me read more slowly, and to discuss ideas with Him as I read. He also brings me the books that have the material I will need immediately for the work that He has for me that day. Eating is pleasant, both in the natural and in the spiritual, but true fitness requires great moderation in each of these areas.

Every Christian has a ministry, or function, in the body of Christ. We are not growing in knowledge and wisdom just to be knowledgeable and wise, but to use them for His glory! We must balance our intake of spiritual food with the exercise of our spiritual gifts and ministries, or even the best spiritual diet

will only cause us to grow fat and lazy spiritually.

Key Principles of Spiritual Development

Beginning with the insights from this analogy, let us consider what determines our rate of spiritual development. What are some of the key principles involved, and what can we expect in practice?

We are called to enter the kingdom of heaven as a little child (see Matthew 18:3). Children receive responsibility a little at a time. One of the main jobs of parenting is to make sure that these new responsibilities are added neither too quickly nor too slowly. With our own children, we watch carefully to be sure that the child is not carrying a burden that is too heavy. Our five year old does an excellent job of making his bed during the summer. When school started, we noticed that the mornings were suddenly not joyful for him. The combination of the new demands of school plus the responsibilities at home were too much for him at that time. We prayed about the situation, and the Lord showed us to take back the responsibility of bed-making for a period. When we lessened his load by that small amount his joy returned, and the too-tired look in his eyes went away.

Our heavenly Father watches over our growth much more carefully than we watch out for our children. We need to ask Him for the faith to trust Him with our growth. When we take on every responsibility that passes us by, we are like a small child that wants to carry the whole weight of the household. That child will probably make less progress in overall development.

When we respond to every demand that we hear, we are saying two things: first, that we must take care of our own growth, and second, that the kingdom being brought into being depends on us, rather than on the Lord. We have the example of Jesus. Jesus did not heal everyone that He saw, but did what He saw His Father doing.

One of the primary reasons for burnout is our tendency to take on burdens that the Lord did not give us. His yoke is easy and His burden is light. When our yoke gets too heavy we have somehow departed from His yoke. If we are going to make a mistake, let's make the mistake of letting a demand pass us by, rather than making the mistake of taking on a responsibility that God did not give to us. If the Lord is giving us a new responsibility He will usually make it very clear.

When we are faced with a new demand, we must not assume that we are to take it, but rather take it to the Lord. We should expect to walk in righteousness, peace and joy. If any of these begin to fade from our life we must learn to stop and reevaluate what we are doing.

This does not mean that life will be easy! The time is short and there is much to do! But, even in the toughest workouts He gives us, we will be able to simultaneously experience righteousness, peace and joy as we take only those that He is giving to us. When we work out physically with a good trainer that we trust, the toughest workouts are the most fun, as we learn to feel ourselves getting stronger as we do it.

Test Yourselves

We should also establish a way to measure both our growth and our performance. It has been said that the Western mentality is that of *doing*, while the Eastern mentality is more concerned with *being*. Obviously the Lord is concerned with both. We are called to bear fruit that will remain, and we are called to be conformed to the image of Jesus. How can we measure each of these to be sure that we are staying on the path to both spiritual maturity and the accomplishing of the purposes to which we have been called?

Picture a body builder who loves to do bench presses. Every day he comes to the gym and bench presses great amounts of weight. He feels very strong. Unfortunately, there are other muscles in his body that he is not exercising if he is just bench pressing. As he continues to develop this way he is increasingly likely to injure the weaker muscles. One

God owes no man anything, which makes the fact that He gave us everything even more astounding.

Max Lucado

day he works with a trainer who tests his strength in these weaker muscles—and he can hardly lift any weight. He may then begin to feel like a failure, but he has actually made more true progress by beginning to work the underdeveloped muscles.

One day my husband and I had a terrible time. Every word seemed to lead to irritation and misunderstanding. By the end of the day we were both considering separate vacations, with the other taking a "long walk off of a short pier." We went to the Lord and asked Him what fundamental things were wrong with us that we could have such a horrible day. He gave me the above picture of a body builder, showing me that he wanted to test some of the weaker areas of our marriage so that He could begin to build those areas. Our marriage is actually very strong in other places; but we needed the revelation that came that day—that He wants to reveal weak areas during peaceful times—to allow time for strengthening, so that in times of storms the weak places will not give way. We could then rejoice and thank Him for creating the perfect set of circumstances to expose these weak points, knowing that with His training our marriage will be perfected.

Feedback from God

It is important to seek the Lord for guidance before and during trials, but it is also good to ask Him for feedback after they are over. He will show us where He would have directed our actions differently, and will show us how He would like for us to handle a given situation in the future. We seldom pass

any test with a perfect score, and the enemy will try to make us feel like a complete failure if we were not perfect. The Lord will show us what we have done right, and what we have done wrong, but even the wrongs that He shows us He does so with truth that sets us free, not with condemnation.

As a personal example, one day my family was to travel to meet my husband's parents at our cottage. We were planning to leave soon after my husband came home from the office. I was packing, taking the time to organize the house as I packed. I also received a couple of visitors and faxes, which slowed me down, but I did not think an hour's delay would matter much. When my husband came home, he noticed that we were behind schedule and informed me that he had promised his parents that we would arrive by 7:00 p.m. at the latest. I reacted strongly to this information, and we exchanged some heated words. After a few minutes, we forgave each other and started throwing stuff into the car. We hurriedly stopped at the store to buy what we needed, and arrived 17 minutes late at the cottage. During the drive, which was tense due to the time pressure, we prayed and asked the Lord to manage the situation and to be glorified. I know that the Lord had consistently worked these situations out for me, so I expected that He would do it here. When my husband's parents were furious at our being late, I was devastated, even to the point where I felt that my faith was wounded.

That night, I was too upset to pray about it, but the following day I sought the Lord and asked Him to show me what had happened. He immediately took me back to my reaction when my husband had told me about our impossible 7:00 deadline. Rather than taking the situation to the Lord, I became angry with my husband. The Lord showed me that if I had turned to Him, He would have given me a plan that would have taken off all of the pressure. It turned out that the reason for the 7:00 deadline was that the parents needed to get to the store before it closed. Our 17 minute delay meant that they were five minutes too late. Had I prayed, the Lord would have told me to call them, and I would have been able to pick up what they needed from the store. These ungodly reactions (anger rather than prayer) usually cost us much more than we ever realize, which is usually why He spends so much time working on them.

The Lord is always willing to give us feedback, and when He does it gives us vision for the discipline. He really does discipline us because He loves us. When we submit to the discipline our lives really will be much easier, and more fruitful.

> **If any of you lacks wisdom, he should ask God, who gives generously to all without finding fault, and it will be given to him (James 1:5).**

Remember that no news is good news. If we ask for feedback and He does not tell us anything specific, then we need to believe that we did things right. We are as little children to Him, and the standards He uses when He works with us resemble those we use with our own children. If we get too tired, ask the Lord to show us what we are carrying that is not His burden (the one that He assigned us), or ask Him for more capacity for handling the burdens.

Expected Results of the Lord's Fitness Program

What will happen when we follow this approach, putting ourselves into His hands for our improvement?

1. We will work harder, but it will seem easier, and we will actually be refreshed by the labor (see Matthew 11:28-30).

2. Whatever we do will produce lasting results (see Ecclesiastes 3:14).

3. The Lord will train us in making use of our time and in being efficient.

4. He will increase our endurance physically, spiritually and emotionally.

5. He will give us joy in things that we previously considered to be burdens.

6. He will make surprising resting places for us. Whereas we previously barely made it to our annual vacation, now we will find that in the middle of the busiest places we can find refreshment in Him.

7. Once we have learned to carry our own load, He will create opportunities for us to help others, which will give us great pleasure!

Final Words

The Lord came to give us an abundant life. Abundance speaks of having more than we need, which means that we will all have enough to make us givers. He will put together a life package for us that will accomplish His purposes, but we must allow Him to manage our lives to remove the clutter that is not from Him. The greatest time and effort consuming parts of many of our lives are also the most unfruitful, and unfulfilling parts, which He did not give us to do. How many people have you seen spending hours a week maintaining their yards, but only a few minutes actually enjoying them? How many other things are there in our lives that require constant dusting, cleaning, or other maintenance, but really add nothing to our lives? How many of us are spending 75% of our "free" time maintaining that which gives us less than 5% of our pleasure? God wants to give us His abundance but, as He inferred in the parable of the talents, He wants us to manage what He gives us properly.

We can trust the Lord to manage our lives much better than we will do on our own. If He calls us to home school our children, He will not simultaneously call us to eight hours a day of intercessory prayer. He knows how many hours there are in a day! If He calls us to missions, He will give us the grace to have our children in the field without their being harmed or hindered. If He calls us to do the impossible, He will give us grace and faith to receive a miracle.

The times that are coming will require that we all be in top shape spiritually, as well as physically. We need to begin moving forward, but we must do this with the wisdom of our Trainer. Let us cease walking in our own wisdom, and put ourselves into the hands of our Lord, who is able to complete His work in us. Let us stop wasting time trying to do everything, and receive our own assignments. Those who will humble themselves to become as little children, God will delight and amaze with spiritual growth beyond their greatest dreams. ■

All Scripture references NIV unless otherwise indicated.

Dr. Suzanne de Treville teaches and consults internationally in the area of manufacturing and strategy. She received her doctorate in business from the Harvard Business School. This is her first article on a Christian topic. She lives in Switzerland with her husband and two children.

THE HARDENING OF BLESSING

Miles Wylie Albright

All Scripture references NIV unless otherwise indicated.

Blessing and calamity must be discerned with the mind of Christ lest we interpret wrongly certain actions of the Lord and doom ourselves by not understanding His ways. To that end, God being my help, I write concerning *the hardening of blessing*.

Recently I was in a spirited charismatic prayer meeting, where we had been praying for healing, restoration, new jobs and other provisions for a whole list of folks. In the midst of this the Lord spoke to me and said, "You really don't want me to do what you're asking." In a matter of two minutes, He took me through the following passages of Scriptures as an explanation.

In Exodus 15, the Israelites, with the glory of the Red Sea deliverance fresh in their minds, take a three day journey into the desert without finding any water. In the desert, three days without water is reaching the point of death. Their lips were parched and their throats were dry. Crying children and bawling livestock added to the bedlam. The pillar of fire that led them was smelting their hearts. Then . . . Glory! Hallelujah! They sight a spring! But when they found it to be bitter, they became likewise bitter; and voiced their complaint to God. How great was the Red Sea deliverance? Great. How big was this test immediately afterward? Big.

They might have foreseen that the Lord would not allow them to die of thirst, though He took them to the brink. But when their faith failed, bitterness blossomed, and the sweet waters of Marah caused the bloom to flourish. If you give a child a treat while he's having a tantrum, his heart is hardened and his misbehavior is increased in all likelihood. Consequently, when in the next chapter we find them being tested less severely, the Israelites complain even more bitterly to God.

This time, although they were driving herds, they complained of having no meat. When God sent quail, they were then convinced that they had discovered how to "write their ticket with God"—by griping and complaining! It was at this point that the Lord introduced Israel to the Sabbath. His purpose was that the people be forced to be still and consider what they were about to do—become permanently hardened. And, despite the forced intermission of Sabbaths, that was exactly what did happen.

The third time that Israel faced a test they passed the point of no return. This time they were out of water again, and they not only began complaining, but they decided to stone Moses as well. David, looking back at this day 500 years later, prophetically interpreted that after this point at Massah-Meribah, Israel had lost the opportunity to enter the Lord's rest. Their hearts had been hardened; the case was closed (see Psalm 95).

I will give them a heart to know me, that I am the Lord. They will be my people, and I will be their God, for they will return to me with all their heart (Jeremiah 24:7).

We remember, sometimes with a wince, that God said He would "harden Pharaoh's heart." We quickly point to the verses that say Pharaoh hardened his own heart. But now we can see that both are true. God blesses Pharaoh with relief from the plagues while his heart was yet unbroken. Because he was not contrite, God's blessing of deliverance didn't really bless Pharaoh, it cursed him. Each time he claimed to submit to God, but in reality he was just physically overmastered by the plagues. Therefore his heart became harder when the plagues were removed.

When Israel first stumbled at Marah God warned them that He could only be their healer, delivering them from the diseases of Egypt, if their hearts were fully committed to Him (see Exodus 15:26). Otherwise, He would be hardening them, as Pharaoh had been by his premature deliverance.

When Jesus fed the 5000, they were a motley crew that had only been with Him one day. His blessing of food turned them into a demanding, manipulative mob that tried to coerce Him into kingship and another meal. Rebuked by the Lord, they began to leave. Looking

---

There is a moment between intending to pray and actually praying that is as dark and silent as any moment in our lives. It is the split second between thinking about prayer and really praying. For some of us, that split second may last for decades.

Emilie Griffin

at the twelve Jesus said, **"Have I not chosen you, the Twelve? Yet one of you is a devil!" (John 6:70).** How did Jesus know that one of the inner circle would be hardened into betrayal? And why did Jesus choose this moment to mention it? He knew Judas' heart was far from contrite. And in that state he had been given the power to heal every disease and sickness, to cast out devils and to raise the dead. He had been hardened by Jesus' unconditional blessing.

Have you ever noticed that Jesus did not seem too pleased with the fruit of the healing of the ten lepers? Do we know why? When crowds of the sick were about to stampede Jesus in Mark 3, He climbed in a boat. Why didn't He simply heal them, en masse? We sing, "Oh, Lord send the power just now," and wonder why He doesn't. If the blessing of power gifts brought Judas a

deadly hardening, we'd better be broken before we're blessed with power, lest one day we cry, "Lord, did we not cast out devils in your name?" Whence comes the anti-Christ? Probably from the ranks of those seeking to do signs and wonders with hearts unyielded. Hence, the lying signs and wonders of the man of sin and the power of God's delusion for those who "do not love the truth" *with all their hearts.*

The Father is the Author of every good gift, but His judgment of "good" is from the Tree of Life. He is too wise to prosper the man whose prosperity will put a hook in his jaw and make him less intimate with the Lord. Only as our souls prosper may He prosper us (see III John 2).

The gospel preaching of the last days will not be in word only, but with power. We think we're waiting for Him to give it. Wrong. He's waiting for us to get to the place where we won't receive the hardening of blessing. ∎

Miles Wylie Albright is the President and Founder of *Day's Dawn Ministries,* one of the pastors of *Open Door Fellowship,* and a stock farmer. He and his wife Barbara have three daughters, Spring Robin, Abigayl Grace and Mary Ruth. They reside in Baileyton, AL.

HE WILL COME TO US LIKE THE RAIN

by

Paul Cain *with Rick Joyner*

All Scripture references NAS unless otherwise indicated.

So let us know, let us press on to know the LORD. His going forth is as certain as the dawn; and He will come to us like the rain, like the spring rain watering the earth (Hosea 6:3).

Every living thing requires water in order to live. Water is provided to us through rain, which is channeled into rivers, streams and lakes. The presence of the Lord is likewise essential for life. As Paul explained to the philosophers of Athens, **"for in Him we live and move and have our being" (Acts 17:28 NKJV).** Even those who do not know Him depend on Him for every breath. The Lord Jesus declared in the Sermon on the Mount, **"for He causes His sun to rise on the evil and the good, and sends rain on the righteous and the unrighteous" (Matthew 5:45).** Even though the Lord blesses all with His omni-presence, those who know Him ever hunger for more of His manifest presence. As the Scripture in Hosea 6:3 states, if we understand how rain comes we can better understand how the Lord comes.

The process by which rain is formed is called the HYDROLOGICAL CYCLE. In the natural process the sun shines upon the oceans, lakes and rivers. The heat causes evaporation, which rises into the air mass to form clouds. This heat also causes the wind to blow which stirs up the dust of the earth. As the vapors rise they cool down and begin to condense around the dust particles to form raindrops. When these drops become too heavy for the clouds to contain, they return to the earth in the form of rain.

Rain softens the soil and provides the essential elements to make the earth fruitful, providing **"seed to the sower and bread to the eater"** as Isaiah 55:10 says. The rain that does not soak into the ground runs into streams and rivers, which run into the lakes and the oceans to start the process all over again.

The spiritual realm has its own hydrological cycle. God's blessings are shining upon us just as the sun shines upon the waters. His blessings warm our hearts and cause us to praise Him out of gratitude. Sometimes God must turn up the heat of circumstances to get us to pray out of necessity, but the purpose is to fill the heavens with more prayer and praise so that the rains will be greater. Our praises, prayers and righteous acts rise to God like the vapors that are created by the sun upon the waters. This worship and intercession forms clouds as it condenses in the heavens. At the same time God causes the winds of the Holy Spirit to blow as He did on the Day of Pentecost, which stirs up men.

Because God made man from the dust of the earth, dust often speaks of our basic, earthly nature. When our worship and prayers combine with the dust to accumulate in the heavens, the rain begins to fall. As the proportion of evaporation determines the amount of rain, so the proportion of our worship and intercession will determine the degree of spiritual rain that we experience. The following Scriptures address aspects of this same truth.

And I will make them and the places round about my hill a blessing; and I will cause the shower to come down in his season; there shall be showers of blessing (Ezekiel 34:26 KJV).

For He maketh small the drops of water: they pour down rain according [in proportion] to the vapor thereof: which the clouds do drop and distil upon man abundantly. Also, can any understand the spreading of the clouds, or the noise of his tabernacle? Behold, he spreadeth his light upon it, and covereth the bottom of the sea (Job 36:27-30 KJV).

Seek Him that maketh the seven stars and Orion, and turneth the shadow of death into the morning, and maketh the day dark with night: that calleth for the waters of the sea, and poureth them out upon the face of the earth: The LORD is his name (Amos 5:8 KJV).

Drop down, ye heavens, from above, and let the skies pour down righteousness: let the earth open, and let them bring forth salvation (Isaiah 45:8 KJV).

Be patient therefore, brethren, unto the coming of the Lord. Behold, the husbandman waiteth for the precious fruit of the earth, and hath long patience for it, until he receive the early and latter rain (James 5:7 KJV).

So rejoice, O sons of Zion, and be glad in the LORD your God; for He has given you the early rain for your vindication. And He has poured down for you the rain, the early and latter rain as before (Joel 2:23).

These Scriptures reveal that there will be an end-time outpouring of the Holy Spirit before the coming of the Lord. That period will be known as the time of the latter rain (see Zechariah 10:1). The Holy Spirit will fall from heaven like a mighty deluge of rain. Joel predicted an unprecedented outpouring of the former and latter rain together (see Joel 2:23). Combine these thoughts with Peter's amazing exhortation that we should be **"looking for *and hastening* the coming of the day of God" (II Peter 3:12).** Could it be that our diligence in prayer, worship and righteous deeds could hasten the coming of the Lord? Could we so fill the spiritual atmosphere that it can hold no more and the rains must begin? The Scriptures indicate that we can.

Once we understand the spiritual hydrological cycle it gives even more impetus to our worship. What is true for the whole earth is also true for our individual lives and congregations. The more we worship Him personally, the more that the personal blessing of His presence will come to us. The more we worship Him as a congregation, the greater the outpouring on our congregation.

It is also a fact that the greatest concentration of rain comes from storms. Storms play a very important part in nature. Their winds are used to bring about a natural pruning of trees. Fires caused by lightning are an important part of nature's own cultivation process, often consuming over-concentrations of weeds, bushes and brambles to enable a whole new cycle of growth to begin. The heavy concentrations of rain from storms are not used so much to saturate the earth as they are to feed the streams and rivers, without which many animals would perish.

A thunderstorm builds up to the mature stage when its clouds are saturated without lightning. The first strike of lightning is what signals the beginning of the rain. In Scripture, lightning is often used as a symbol for revelation. We see this in Psalm 97:1-6:

The LORD reigns; let the earth rejoice; let the many islands be glad.
Clouds and thick darkness surround Him; righteousness and justice are the foundation of His throne.

Fire goes before Him, and burns up His adversaries round about.

His lightnings lit up the world; the earth saw and trembled.

The mountains melted like wax at the presence of the LORD, at the presence of the Lord of the whole earth.

The heavens declare His righteousness, and all the peoples have seen His glory.

Understanding that the heavens declare His righteousness, the psalmist is here using the storm as a metaphor to describe how the presence of the Lord comes. Just as lightning can reveal everything that is hidden in darkness, God's revelation does the same, revealing what is hidden in men's hearts. Just as a lightning strike usually signals the beginning of the rain, it has been a revelation from God that has started almost every outpouring of the Holy Spirit or revival. It was the illumination by revelation upon the book of Romans to Martin Luther that ignited the Reformation, and every great move that followed came by a similar revelation of God's truth from the Scriptures.

It is also noteworthy that a lightning strike that touches the earth has its origin on earth. There is a buildup of negative charges that attract the positive charge from the storm. If you have ever been very close to a lightning strike you can feel the atmosphere become charged *before* the strike. The same is true before the revelation of God strikes the earth. The revelation that came to Martin Luther from the book of Romans came

as a result of the deep darkness that had come upon the church during that time. This concentrated and focused men who were committed to change. The following reformation movements, and the great revivals in Scripture and history, all seemed to begin when conditions became so bad on earth that they attracted the power of God and a revelation of His truth to counter it. After the revelation of His truth, or the lightning, a downpour of His rain, or teaching, would follow.

The same can be true in our congregations, families, or individual lives. When the enemy releases such a concentration of negative "charges" in our lives, it actually attracts the positive charge from heaven, and then releases His rain in our life. This can also be true in relation to spiritual hunger. When there is a great enough concentration of those who are desperate for God, who are "poor in spirit," God is moved to send His revelation and the rain of His blessings and presence.

Hindrances to Blessings

If we believe that the Scriptures teach that we can help determine the amount of blessing that we receive, and even hasten the coming of the Lord, then we must also recognize the things that will hinder the release of the rain of God. One of the obvious hindrances is sin. **"If I regard iniquity in my heart, the Lord will not hear me" (Psalm 66:18 KJV).** We cannot expect worship to compensate for presumptuous sin in our lives. Here we are talking about willful disobedience rather than the common stumblings of immaturity and weakness.

Another hindrance can be condemnation. The Lord freely gives His provision to His children, but we must extend our faith to receive it. Condemnation attacks the very foundation of our faith that God really wants us to have His provision. A person under condemnation will be self-centered instead of God-centered. Such a person can be given a checkbook with God's endless resources deposited in the account, but they will not write any checks because they cannot believe that there is anything in *their* account.

There is therefore now no condemnation to them which are in Christ Jesus, who walk not after the flesh, but after the Spirit (Romans 8:1 KJV).

Another spiritual stronghold that can keep us from receiving the blessings of God is "worldliness." I once heard a man say, "Worldliness is everything that cools my affections toward God." The Scriptures portray worldliness as the opposite of spirituality. Worldliness is focusing on the temporary realm in place of the eternal purposes of God. As the Lord explained in the parable of the sower, such cares choke out the word of God.

> Just as lightning can reveal everything that is hidden in darkness, God's revelation does the same, revealing what is hidden in men's hearts.

Another hindrance to our receiving the blessings or provision of God can be our wrong concepts of Him. This is a form of deception, the veil that the enemy places over the hearts of men to keep them from walking in the purposes of God. Wrong concepts of God can be either seeing Him as too harsh, or seeing Him as too soft. That is why Paul exhorted us to, **"behold then the kindness and severity of God" (Romans 11:22).** We must behold both His kindness and His severity to know Him as He is. If we just look at one aspect or the other, we will be deceived about His true nature. God does not ever want to condemn us. He truly desires that all men would be saved and come to the knowledge of the truth, but He will not compromise His standards of holiness in order to accommodate us. He is holy and we must be holy if we are to walk with Him. However, when we do fail we must learn to run to Him and not away from Him. He may discipline us but He will only do what is good for us.

Religious traditions can also be a hindrance to our receiving the blessings of God. No demon, principality or power, not even Satan himself, can stand before the Word of God, but Jesus said to the Pharisees: **"You have made the commandment of God of no effect by your tradition" (Matthew 15:6 NKJV).** Just think of that! Our traditions can accomplish what the demons of hell cannot do! Redemption releases; religion represses. The primary effect of religious traditions that are of human origin is to stop the free-flowing life of God in the church and channel men's efforts and affections into dead works. Not all traditions are bad, as Paul exhorted the churches to hold fast to the traditions that he had delivered to them. However, many traditions have become to the church what the "high places" were to Israel. It was written that many of the kings in Israel stumbled because they did not tear down the high places. These were places they had erected to offer sacrifices to God that were more convenient than going down to the temple. However, God had not prescribed these places, or many of the sacrifices that they offered on them, so He would not receive them. These also kept the people from going down to the temple to worship Him in the way that He had prescribed. As will always happen with such compromises, soon they were offering sacrifices to other gods on these altars. There are many traditions that now seem to be an integral part of Christianity, but actually are not biblical practices. These may seem harmless, and some even seem to be important, but their effect is to keep us occupied with something that is at best less than the perfect will of God. We actually have some traditions in the church that are like severed arteries that are draining the very life-blood from the body.

Another obvious stumbling block to the blessings of God is pride. James 4:6 (NKJV) states, **"God resists the proud, but gives grace to the humble."** Some stumble because they become proud when they are blessed by God, starting to think that the blessings come because of their righteousness. This has been especially true during times of revival. God sends revival because the people are hungry enough and humble enough to cry out to Him. Then they become proud, thinking that the revival came because they were so spiritual, or were doing everything just right. Then the Lord has to remove, and sometimes even resist, the revival because of the pride of the people. This same thing can happen when we receive anything from God. **"The proud He knows from afar" (Psalm 138:6 NKJV).**

The fear of man can be another stumbling block that keeps us from receiving, or keeping, the blessings of God. In John 5:44 (NKJV), Jesus said: **"How can you believe, who receive honor from one another, and do not seek the honor that comes from the only God?"** We receive from God because we have faith in Him. When we begin to seek the honor, or recognition, of men, we are starting to put our faith in men, which the Scriptures clearly warn us against. We should be neither encouraged or discouraged because of what men think of us. Proverbs 29:25 (NKJV) says, **"The fear of man brings a snare, but whoever trusts in the LORD shall be safe."** The true fear of God displaces the fear of man (see Proverbs 9:10).

Satanic oppression can be another hindrance to the flow of God's blessing and presence in our lives. He does set up strongholds to try to thwart God's purposes. We see in the book of Daniel how an angelic messenger who had been sent to Daniel was held up for twenty-one days by "the prince of the kingdom of Persia" until Michael came to help him (see Daniel 10:13). Of course, Satan and all of his hosts could not hinder a messenger of God for a single moment if God did not allow it. When He does allow it, it is to make us stronger. During that twenty-one days Daniel did not faint, but persevered even more in seeking the Lord through prayer and fasting. We must learn to do the same. The blessings of God are for those who desire them enough to seek until they find, knock until the doors are opened. When satanic oppression or hindrance is allowed, we should seek the Lord as to why He is allowing it, but we must never give up because of it.

Just as Satan's prince intercepted the messenger sent to Daniel, one of Satan's primary objectives is to intercept the worship that we offer to God in order to direct it to himself. Satan even tried to turn the worship of the Son of God, saying, **"All these things will I give thee, if thou wilt fall down and worship me" (Matthew 4:9 KJV).** He made this offer to Jesus at the end of a long period of fasting and seeking the Father. What he offered Jesus was an easy way to receive all that He had already been offered by God. God required Him to go to the cross to receive the promises, but Satan was saying all He had to do was bow down and worship him and He could have the world right then. Satanic attacks are often designed to turn us from the true course by seducing us into taking an easier one. Satan will still offer the world to those who will worship him, or do things his way. Getting men to worship him is his primary objective, as we see in Isaiah 14:13-14:

> **For thou hast said in thine heart, I will ascend into heaven, I will exalt my throne above the stars of God.**
>
> **I will ascend above the heights of the clouds: I will be like the most High.**

We must always be wary of anything that diverts our worship, suppresses it, or hinders our joy and freedom in worship. Worship is where we find our highest purpose, and we know that the Lord inhabits the praises of His people (see Psalm 22:3).

What Will Release the Rain?

First of all, we need to acknowledge and thank God for the rain that is already falling. One reason so much divine rain has come to Toronto under the ministry of John Arnott is because he traveled around the world for years having many anointed leaders lay hands on him. These prayers for the anointing accumulated in the heavens until they could hold no more, and the rains came to his church in Toronto. When I think of Toronto, I feel like Elijah's servant when he said, **"Behold, a cloud as small as a man's hand is coming up from the sea" (I Kings 18:44).** The Toronto movement may seem small and insignificant to some, but it is a sure sign of an abundance of rain that is coming.

The rain I have lived for all my life is called the Last Day Ministry. I believe that worship, praise, adoration, prayer and intercession will all help to release this ministry, but one ingredient that I am still looking for, which is just as necessary, is repentance. Just as Peter said,

Repent therefore and return, that your sins may be wiped away, in order that times of refreshing may come from the presence of the Lord (Acts 3:19).

We should be thankful for the rain we are seeing, but not settle for it. Let us raise our prayers continually to cry for more rain. Let us put off everything that hinders, and the sin which so easily besets us, and give ourselves wholly for the great task that has been set before us—to preach the gospel of Jesus Christ to every nation and tribe, and to lift up the Son of God so that all men can be drawn to Him. Let it be said of us as it was of Cornelius, that our prayers and gifts for His service have COME UP for a memorial before Him. As a result, God sent his most eminent apostle there to see to it that Cornelius' entire house was filled with the Holy Spirit. If we will seek Him like Cornelius did, He will also send us His best so that His Spirit may again be released in our midst. ■

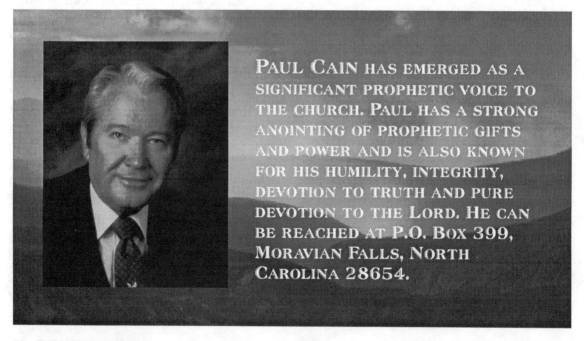

PAUL CAIN HAS EMERGED AS A SIGNIFICANT PROPHETIC VOICE TO THE CHURCH. PAUL HAS A STRONG ANOINTING OF PROPHETIC GIFTS AND POWER AND IS ALSO KNOWN FOR HIS HUMILITY, INTEGRITY, DEVOTION TO TRUTH AND PURE DEVOTION TO THE LORD. HE CAN BE REACHED AT P.O. BOX 399, MORAVIAN FALLS, NORTH CAROLINA 28654.

PROPHECY

THE QUEST

by Rick Joyner

All Scripture references NAS unless otherwise indicated.

Behold, I stand at the door and knock; if anyone hears My voice and opens the door, I will come in to him, and will dine with him, and he with Me (Revelation 3:20).

This Scripture must be one of the great dilemmas for every seeker of God. Here we see the Lord on the outside knocking to be let in to His own church. This should arouse several important questions: Why would Almighty God knock on the door to be let in to His own church? Why does He not just enter? Why is He on the outside? What are the knocks that He is using to get our attention so that we will open the door?

Worship And Liberty

Until we understand the answer to question number one it is unlikely that we will understand the answers to the other questions. God is patiently knocking on the door of His own church because He cannot force Himself on us and still expect us to worship Him in spirit and truth. He will not rape His bride. If He were to force His affections on the church her affections would not be real. He will only come in to dwell with those who desire Him. This is why He placed the Tree of the Knowledge of Good and Evil in the Garden in the first place. There could be no true obedience from the heart unless there was the freedom to disobey. There can be no worship from the heart unless there is the freedom not to worship. When we are pressured to worship, or into obedience, the possibility of either true worship or true obedience is negated.

We know that when the Lord returns He is not going to be so patient. He is coming to rule with a rod of iron. The Lord could have begun such a rule immediately after His resurrection, but He had another purpose. The entire church age has been for the purpose of calling those who would rule and reign with Him. The primary purpose for the church age has been the formation of the church, not the reformation of the world. He has been completing His church in the heavenly places, made up of the overcomers in each generation. That is why His call to the seven churches in Revelation were to the overcomers. Their influence on the earth has brought reform as they have been the salt of the earth, but when the Lord Himself returns with them, the world will be changed, and will become obedient to Him. Even so, after the transformation is complete we see that Satan is released again for a short time in order to prove that their obedience is from the heart.

It may seem contradictory, but for obedience to be from our heart it must *not* be our primary objective. The greatest commandment is to love the Lord, because if we do not obey Him out of love, our obedience will not be from our heart. If we truly love Him we will obey Him, but if we obey Him we may not love Him. If we esteem love above obedience we will obey Him better than if we esteem obedience above love. Obedience can actually become an idol that separates us from God. This will then quickly lead to our serving more in a religious spirit, which seeks to have us base our relationship to God on performance rather than grace.

If all that the Lord desired from His creation was obedience He would have done better to have created the computer instead of man. Then all He would have needed to do was program His computer to worship Him and it would have done it exactly right every time. But could this kind of worship ever be acceptable? Of course not! Then how do we expect our programmed worship to be acceptable? In this I am not just talking about our praise or singing, but all of our service.

As Paul explained, **"Where the Spirit of the Lord is, there is liberty" (II Corinthians 3:17).** The Holy Spirit first and foremost promotes liberty. True obedience is not possible without freedom, and the Father seeks worship that is done in spirit and truth, because we want to, not just because we have to. We can get a parrot to say the right things, and do what we want it to, but it will not be in the parrot's heart. We can get men to say the right things, and even do the right things, but if it is not in their heart it will never please God. The Lord is not just trying to get us to say the right things and comply with certain standards of behavior. He is seeking a people who love Him and love the truth above all things.

This is not to negate the importance of obedience, leadership, or structure in our meetings. Some think that the only way for the Holy Spirit to lead a meeting is for us to come completely open to Him, without plan or agenda. This may work for some, but often these meetings are led more by the immature, the unstable, and the rebellious who quickly step in to fill the leadership void. Leadership and organization do not have to be in conflict with the Holy Spirit. The highest form of worship usually does not come just because we are open for anything, but rather because we have sought the Lord and know ahead of time what He wants to do, and plan accordingly.

The Plan

It is not possible to share a word like this without there being a danger of overreaction on the part of some. For example, many who begin to see the freedom that we must have to walk with God can develop a belief that it is impossible to follow the Holy Spirit if we have any predetermined plans or agendas. Such a mentality is often more in harmony with the spirit of lawlessness than with the Holy Spirit. To use the example of the order that is found in nature, it is not the result of no planning, but of the longest range planning possible—God planned what we are now doing before the foundation of the world! If we are in harmony with the Holy Spirit we, too, should be able to see much farther ahead, and be able to plan accordingly. Planning is a basic part of God's nature, and should be ours, too.

This does not mean that we should be ruled by planning committees, but He wants to give us our plans. When Moses was commissioned to build a dwelling place for the Lord, He gave him specific, detailed plans for it. We, too, must learn to go up on the mountain into His presence to receive our plans from Him. If all who are called to be builders would receive their plans from Him, instead of just copying each other's plans, there would be a great deal more diversity and life in the body of Christ.

Neither should the liberty of the Spirit be interpreted as license to do whatever we want to do. The true liberty of the Spirit is the freedom to follow the Spirit. Some congregations may actually be too free, allowing almost anything out of a fear of missing the Holy Spirit. I have sat through many meetings that were supposedly "led by the Spirit," but were in fact led more by the immature, the unstable, and the rebellious, who quickly filled the void left by the lack of leadership. The fact is that the Holy Spirit is rarely able to do anything in such meetings, or through churches or movements that lack strong decisive leadership.

Peter warned that the "unstable and untaught" were distorting the words of Paul, as well as the rest of the Scriptures, to their own destruction (see II Peter 3:16). We will always have the unstable and untaught among us who will try to dictate the course to their own liking and comfort. To allow them to do this is to be led into the same destruction that they are headed for. The Lord's goal is not to bring us to a place of no leadership in the church, but where the leadership is more fully joined to Him. One of the ultimate conflicts at the end of the age will be with the spirit of lawlessness, and we must not allow it to have its way in the church.

Being "open to the Holy Spirit" does not mean that we walk around perpetually not knowing what to do next, which will only lead to serious instability. Being open to the Spirit does mean that we must always be open to changes, but only to the changes that He wants to make. The Lord Jesus did not go through life never knowing what the Spirit was going to lead Him to do next. He always knew what the Spirit was leading Him to do next. That is how He is calling us to walk. The true freedom of the Spirit comes from knowing clearly what we are called to do, which releases us to go forward with boldness.

There is probably far more evil released and tolerated through the lack of planning than because of wrong planning. There is truth to the proverb that "Those who fail to plan, plan to fail." But our goal must be to plan by the Spirit rather than according to mere human wisdom. It is not wrong to plan worship, or other things that we are called to do. The point of stumbling comes when we try to use the plan as the motivator rather than our love for the Lord. In worship, it is not enough to just do the right things —we must do them for the right reasons. Worship or obedience that is performed out of compulsion, or hype, can be a deception by which we appease our consciences in such a way that we are no longer compelled to seek the reality. As the Lord stated it through Jeremiah:

My people have become lost sheep; their shepherds have led them astray. They have made them turn aside on the mountains; they have gone along from mountain to hill and have forgotten their resting place (Jeremiah 50:6).

There was a point in my ministry when the Lord showed me that I was one of those shepherds who was leading His sheep astray. I was doing it in this same way; leading the people from one high place to the next, from project to project, hype to hype, always keeping them

moving and trying to keep them excited, but not leading them to their resting place in intimate relationship with the Lord Himself. This is possibly the primary reason for the Laodicean spirit of luke-warmness in the church today—she is simply weary of going from project to project but never really connecting to the Lord. We "lead people to the Lord," but somehow all they ever get is us!

When the church becomes intimate with the Lord, and labors with Him, taking His yoke, instead of laboring for Him, she will find such rest and refreshment in His presence that she will be able to do much more than she can now. Possibly the number one reason for burnout and weariness in the church today has been our tendency to take the people's yokes instead of the Lord's yoke. Jesus never responded to human need; He only did what He saw the Father doing. Until we learn the same, we may be caught up in a lot of labor, but we will not be doing the work of God.

God's Second Book

A second major ingredient in true worship is diversity. God's diversity is much more profound than just changing the songs we sing. Jon Amos Comenius called nature "God's second book." This was essentially what Paul said in Romans 1:20:

For since the creation of the world His invisible attributes, His eternal power and divine nature, have been clearly seen, being understood through what has been made, so that they are without excuse.

Everything that was made reflects the Creator. The awesome diversity of the creation reflects one of the basic attributes of our Creator—He is creative! He makes every snowflake different. There are no two trees in the world exactly alike. He made every human being unique and different. If this is such a basic characteristic of His creation, why is it that the church, which is supposed to be the embodiment of His nature and ways, is so boringly uniform?

Why is it that we try to make every congregation alike. Why do our church meetings tend to always follow the same pattern? How is the church, supposedly the dwelling place of our glorious Creator, so devoid of creativity? Possibly the greatest threat to the church today is not persecution from liberals, or even sin, but terminal boredom. What we often call church planting is nothing more than franchising, which have more in common with Burger King than the King of Kings. Mistaking uniformity for obedience may well prove to have been one of the church's most devastating mistakes.

We claim that God is a God of order, and He is, but His order is very different from our typical human concept of order. The basic human concept of order is uniformity. We like straight rows, singing in harmony, everyone in the choir wearing the same color robes, and everything else very neat and tidy. However, if you want to see God's order, take a walk through the woods. There are no straight lines in nature. There seems to be no system to the way all kinds of different trees and plants grow up right next to each other. It looks like chaos, but there is an order in nature that is so intricate that no human mind has yet fathomed it. What looks to the human mind as chaos is an order and harmony far beyond our comprehension.

Having our chairs in straight rows and a devotion to neatness is not necessarily contrary to God's order. In most cases it is just practical. Even so, we must understand that this in itself does not reflect God's order. The Lord Jesus, who was in perfect obedience to the Father, never seemed to do anything the same way twice. He healed many different people, but almost every time He used a new procedure. Both His messages and the settings in which He gave them changed daily. He was so diverse in His ministry that John finally wrote that if everything that He did had been written that even the world itself could not have contained the books. How is it that the people who are supposed to be conformed to the image of the Prince of Life are so lifeless, void of creativity, and predictable?

The New Testament Is Not Just Another Law

One of the primary reasons for this bondage to uniformity in the church has been the subtle theology promoted by many which essentially teaches that the New Testament is just another law. The New Testament was not given to be another law, but to free us from the yoke of the law. The law can never make men righteous or acceptable to God. The New Testament was not given to constrain us not to do anything that was not written in it, but rather to free us to do whatever is not directly forbidden by it. There is a fundamental difference in these two approaches which is nothing less than the same conflict that existed in the Garden by which we must choose between the Tree of the Knowledge of Good and Evil and the Tree of Life.

This does not imply that everything that we do that is not in direct conflict with the New Testament is right, but it forces us to seek a living relationship to the Lord so that we follow Him as He did the Father. We must know and follow the Holy Spirit, who was given to lead us into all truth. **"For the letter kills, but the Spirit gives life" (II Corinthians 3:6).** We should search the New Testament to understand and apply the wisdom of the methods and principles laid out by its authors. However, we are free to try that which is not directly forbidden, or indirectly implied as being evil. Walking in truth is more than just understanding doctrines properly. Truth is a Person, and walking in Truth is to abide in Him. We will only stay on the path of life to the degree that we are doing that which we see the Spirit doing, just as Jesus lived by doing what He saw the Father doing.

As quoted, **"Now the Lord is the Spirit; and where the Spirit of the Lord is, there is liberty" (II Corinthians 3:17).** A more literal translation of this could be, "Where the Spirit is Lord, there is liberty." The Holy Spirit really does promote liberty above obedience. This is not because obedience is not important, but because true obedience from the heart is not possible unless there is liberty. Only when there is true liberty can there ever be true unity. True unity is not found just in uniformity. The only place where we can now find unity in uniformity among men is in the cemetery. The closer we are to that ideal of unity the closer to being dead we are.

The Scriptures are a most precious gift, and essential for the reproof of our doctrines and practices, but the New Testament was meant to set us free to follow the Spirit, not bind us with another Law. The Lord never said that when He went away we would be comforted and led into all truth by the book that He was sending us, but by the Spirit. The Scriptures have been tragically misused when they are used to usurp the Holy Spirit's place in our life. As Francis Frangipane likes to say, true Christianity is not following a manual, but rather following Immanuel. True Christianity is a reunion and relationship with our blessed Creator, not just learning to follow a book of procedure.

We must never disregard the Scriptures, which is an obvious and foolish overreaction. They would not have been given to us if they were not important. The Lord Jesus Himself took His stands and defended His positions with, "It is written." However, we must use the Scriptures properly, and keep their use within their intended parameters, or that which was meant for good will only become an idol and stumbling block to us. As even the secular historian Will Durant perceived, if there were no guidelines along which our minds can travel with unconscious ease, we would become perpetually hesitant and ultimately reduced to insanity. The Scriptures give us general guidelines that keep us safe, but also are broad enough to free us to each seek Him, and relate to Him in a unique and special relationship.

The Unholy War

It is true that those who fail to esteem the Scriptures properly will end up just as deceived, and probably more demented and perverted, than those who wrongly replace the Holy Spirit with the Scriptures. If we had to choose one form of deception I would choose the one that esteemed the Scriptures beyond their proper place, but the path that leads to life is not found in either of these extremes. With one extreme we will end up dead because of the letter that kills. With the other extreme we end up dead in transgressions, but with both we will end up equally dead.

As the Lord explained, **"Ye do err, not knowing the scriptures, nor the power of God" (Matthew 22:29 KJV).** Presently, those who know the Scriptures tend to err because they do not know the power of God, and those who know the power of God tend to err because they do not know the Scriptures. The Lord has called us to walk in truth by properly knowing the Scriptures and the power of God. There is presently a great blending of these emphases, or overemphases if that is the case, that presents the greatest hope for the church since the first century.

The conflict between those who devote themselves to the Scriptures without knowing the power, or those who devote themselves mostly to the power without knowing the Scriptures well, is the basic conflict in the church between the prophetic/evangelist types and the pastor/teacher types. Both have essential truth, and both sides will remain in essential error until the conflict is ended. God ordained that all of these ministries are required for the proper equipping of His church. The Scriptures make it clear that all of these ministries, along with the apostle, are given *"**until** we all attain to **the unity of the faith, and of the knowledge of the Son of God, to a mature man, to the measure of the stature which belongs to the fulness of Christ"** (Ephesians 4:13).* Is there a church anywhere in the world that measures up to this? Then obviously all of these ministries are still needed.

The Lord is going to restore true apostolic Christianity to the earth. To do this He is going to have to restore true apostles to the church. We cannot expect this until the prophets and teachers learn to worship the Lord together just as they did at Antioch. When they did this the Lord released possibly the two greatest missionary apostles of all time—Paul and Barnabas. The war between these ministries must end, and it will. The churches and movements that end it first will be the first to cross the barrier into the final phase of church history. When this happens all of the gifts and ministries in the church will rise to their proper place.

Is There Nothing New?

One of the tragic misunderstandings of people who seek to be biblical is from Solomon's statement, **"That which has been is that which will be, and that which has been done is that which will be done. So, there is nothing new**

under the sun" (Ecclesiastes 1:9). There are historic and general senses in which this statement is true, but taken to the extreme beyond what it was intended to mean, will lead to a profound deception. The "new creation" itself was instituted by God after this statement was made. In fact, who could even count the many inventions and new things created since this statement was done? Our daily life is probably filled with more new things and experiences than we can count.

To understand the Book of Ecclesiastes we must understand that it is written from the position of being "under the sun," or from the earthly, human perspective. This is an important book in the canon of Scripture because it reveals perceptions that men have when they are not able to see from the heavenly perspective. For example, this book declares that men are just beasts with no eternal destiny (see Ecclesiastes 3:18-22). This is not true, but it shows the limit of our view when we can only see things "from under the sun."

When this wrong concept that there is nothing new is applied to worship, or our faith, it imposes a stagnation that will quickly dry up the rivers of life that are supposed to be flowing through us. One reason that the living water is found in a river, and not a pond or lake, is because living water is flowing, going somewhere. It has been said that "You can never step into the same river twice." Because a river flows it is constantly changing both its own path and the landscape around it. The Lord used the metaphor of water for truth, because truth, like water, must flow in order to stay pure. If it stops flowing it will stagnate very fast.

It was the mind-set of sameness and rigidity in worship that the Lord rejected, saying, **"Because this people draw near with their words and honor Me with their lip service, but they remove their hearts far from Me, and *their reverence for Me consists of tradition learned by rote"* (Isaiah 29:13).** His exhortation was to, **"Sing to the Lord a *new* song" (Isaiah 42:10).** In other places the Lord promised to put a new spirit within us (see Ezekiel 11:19); to do a new thing (see Isaiah 43:19); to give us, **"a new**

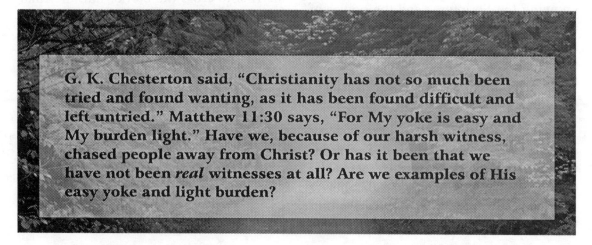

G. K. Chesterton said, "Christianity has not so much been tried and found wanting, as it has been found difficult and left untried." Matthew 11:30 says, "For My yoke is easy and My burden light." Have we, because of our harsh witness, chased people away from Christ? Or has it been that we have not been *real* witnesses at all? Are we examples of His easy yoke and light burden?

commandment" (John 13:34); to make us, "new creatures" (II Corinthians 5:17); and He "inaugurated a new and living way" (Hebrews 10:20); and when we are born again, "all things become new" (II Corinthians 5:17); and we are to walk in "the newness of life" (Romans 6:4). Ultimately the Lord is going to make "all things new" (Revelation 21:5). The overwhelming testimony of the Scriptures is that God does many new things. Those who wrongly understand the one statement, "There is nothing new under the sun," have inevitably been those who were the most prone to miss what God is presently doing.

As Jeremiah observed, "His compassions . . . are *new* every morning" (Lamentations 3:22-23). Just as He revealed His mercy in a new way every day that He walked the earth, He is constantly showing His mercy in new ways with each of us. A wife may love flowers, but if her husband brought home the same type of bouquet everyday she would soon get bored with it. Our God is the greatest Lover who knows how to keep the relationship with His bride fresh. One of the most devastating errors to come upon the church in every age has come through submitting to the pressure to conform, or to measure God's order by uniformity.

Satan's Cord of Three Strands

Satan also has a cord of three strands which is not easily broken. It is composed of the religious spirit, the control spirit, and the political spirit. As stated, the religious spirit seeks to have us base our spirituality on the performance of religious duties rather than by seeking a relationship with our Redeemer. The control spirit works with the religious spirit to impose compliance, even with biblical standards, but a compliance imposed by external pressure rather than by the Spirit through a change of heart. The political spirit empowers the first two by having us focus our attention on what men think rather than what God thinks. Satan has effectively used this cord to bind almost every new movement to date. The movement which effectively resists these attacks will unquestionably have the greatest potential for fully crossing over into the Promised Land that has been given to us in Christ.

Every new movement in the church has suffered a massive assault from the "thought police" who try to rob the movement of its freshness, and the people of their liberty in Christ. This is one of Satan's most effective ways to divert men from the essence of the true faith, a living relationship with God. In this way a true faith is replaced by mere rituals and formulas that make men into automatons who simply seek to conform and fit in. Soon men are not seeking to conform to the image of Christ as much as they are seeking to conform to the image of the leaders of the movement. Even the newest and freshest forms of worship are quickly turned into new traditions which stringently resist further innovation or change. This will continue until we fully comprehend that our God is the Creator who will always be ultimately and profoundly creative. When we are truly joined to Him we will be the same.

God does not change and this nature has never changed. When He created man in His image one of the most basic characteristics of that image was creativity. When we have been fully delivered from the yoke of bondage, creativity will abound in us like never before. When the church is fully freed from the yoke of Satan's cord of three strands, the church will become the very center of creativity, and science, on the earth. *True* science will always lead to the Creator. *True* art will always reveal Christ, through whom and for whom all things were made, and in whom all things will be summed up.

When the church enters into true worship, she will produce the greatest scientists and the greatest artists that the world has ever seen. The Lord knows all things. The gift of a word of knowledge is simply a brief touch of the mind of Christ who knows all things. When we are fully joined to the mind of Christ we will be getting much more than people's names and addresses! This may be a good start, but we must go on from here. The more that we are joined to Him, and have His mind, the more that the very secrets of the universe will be opened to us—past, present and future.

Resisting Religious Socialism

Socialism is dying or is in retreat almost everywhere, but in the church! Socialism was one of the ultimate manifestations of Satan's cord of three strands. It sought to shape everyone into the same mold. This cut off the creative, individual character of man that is essential to the image of God in man that is to be recovered by redemption. Socialism essentially makes the institution the source, which removes both initiative and responsibility from men—both of which kill creativity. As the socialistic governments collapse, there will be a strong tendency for the church to try to take their place in providing many social needs. This is a deadly trap! The church is not the source, but is here to point men to the Source—Jesus. Jesus Christ really is the answer to every human problem, and can supply every human need. However, if the church tries to be the Holy Spirit to people, the very power of her gospel message will be diluted accordingly.

The church does have a place in being a vessel through whom the Lord can reach to touch the needs of His people. However, we must be very careful not to take the people's yokes, but only do that which the Lord is leading us to do. Only then will He do the works through us. Without Him we will fail just as tragically as the socialist governments. The Lord could wave His hand and meet the needs of the whole world for all time, but He is obviously not doing this for a reason. Sometimes, not doing what we have not been called to do is harder than doing what we have been called to do. True obedience, and true worship, require this resolve.

Living In the NEW Creation

"New" is a word greatly feared by the rigid and insecure. However, those who talk the most about God doing a new thing are often those who are the most resistant to change. This tendency is called by psychologists "presenting a bold exterior in order to hide corruption on the inside." This principle is why those who become the most vehement attackers of others are almost always found to be hiding serious sins of their own. Those who are the most rigid sticklers for doctrinal purity are often those who are the most prone to serious license with the Scriptures. This is why Paul told Timothy to, **"Pay attention to your own teachings" (I Timothy 4:16).**

If you want to know what God is saying to almost any preacher, listen to his preaching. It has been the nature of the church to preach many things that we need to hear first and foremost. Possibly the most radical new thing that the world could ever witness would be a church that actually lives what it preaches. The new thing that God is trying to do in us is not a new truth, but a fresh revelation of the age old gospel, a revelation so real that we will really live by it. We must have fresh manna daily if we are going to make it to our promised land. That Manna is Jesus Christ.

When the author of Hebrews exhorted to **"leave the elementary teachings about the Christ" (Hebrews 6:1),** he did not mean that we should leave the teachings about Christ, but rather the *elementary* teachings about Him. We must need to go on to the deeper revelations of Christ. What does it mean that He is a priest according to the Order of Melchizedek? The Book of Hebrews is considered the deepest and most profound of the New Testament, but the author rebuked his readers because they should have been eating meat and he could only give them what he considered "milk" for spiritual babies (see Hebrews 5:12-14). How are we ever going to eat meat if we cannot even digest what the New Testament considers milk? Yet that same New Testament book exhorts us to leave the elementary teachings and go on.

Jesus is no longer a carpenter from Nazareth. He is a King beyond our comprehension of what a King is. He dwells in glory beyond any earthly comprehension of glory. The riches of His wisdom are beyond our limited ability to comprehend. As stated, we are impressed when we get someone's name or physical affliction by a word of knowledge, and we should be because this is wonderful. Even so, we must understand that there is much more available. The Lord upholds the universe by the word of His power. He has unlimited knowledge of each person on earth, and if we become of one mind with Him, the supernatural knowledge that we have access to will greatly transcend what we are touching now. Let us not despise the small beginnings, but let us also understand that we are far from walking in all that God has made available to us by His Holy Spirit. The power of the One who created all things lives within everyone of us! We are supposed to be seated with Him in the heavenly places (see Ephesians 2:6). What would the world really look like from that perspective? Before the end there will be a people who will find out.

We are now coming to the time when new moves of God will be arising at a pace we have never witnessed before.

This is going to happen because men are going to break the shackles that the timid and visionless have placed upon Christianity. They will have little regard for what religious men might think of them, or say about them. New congregations will be springing up almost everywhere. God is about to make a frontal assault on the delusion of His church that has kept it so captive to the pressures of conformity and uniformity. He really is going to renew our minds. Those who experience His mercy in a new way every morning will be made new every morning, and they will begin to bring continual new birth to the world. They will have such security in their relationship to Him that they will be able to embrace the new things that He is doing without the present paranoia that so dominates the church.

This will be a most unsettling time for those who are bound by Satan's cord of three strands. To the rest it will be like the coming of the bluest sky after the longest of storms. The very definition that men have given to Christianity will change over the next few years. What is coming, the world will not be able to put into its neat little categories for religion. The world is about to be filled with marvel and wonder at what it sees and hears coming from the church. This will become such an interest to the world that church news will become a constant part of the national and international news. When true worship is released in the church, our meetings will become more interesting than sports or concerts of the now popular "idols."

True worship touches the heart of man like nothing else can because it touches the heart of God. We were created for His pleasure, and there is nothing more fulfilling for the human soul than fulfilling this purpose. As the church becomes what she was created to be, the world will witness the most secure, fulfilled and creative people it has ever seen. Even though there will be so many new movements arising, they will flow together in a harmony that no power of man could have controlled. The church will become the greatest revelation of the symphony of God's great diversity, and it will capture the attention and imagination of the entire world.

The Boast of Satan

Early in Israel's journey from Egypt, the people fell into such debauchery that the Lord threatened to destroy them all except Moses. Moses interceded for the people by declaring that if the Lord destroyed them the whole world would believe that God had the power to deliver the people out of Egypt, but He did not have the power to bring them into the Promised Land. God listened to Moses and patiently waited for that generation to pass away, and then led the next generation into the Promised Land.

Today Satan boasts that even though God can redeem men, He cannot change them. Before the end comes, God will have the witness of a church on the earth that is not only redeemed, but changed. His church will not continue to reflect the evils of the world, but will be changed into the image of His Son. Before the end there will be a church without spot or wrinkle. That it is without spot, speaks of her purity. That it is without wrinkle, speaks of her perpetual youthfulness. The bride will have made herself ready for the bridegroom, and the world and devils will no longer have the boast that the church is no different from them.

Born for Greatness

There is one common characteristic by which men or events are judged "great"—they are unique. Uniqueness does not necessarily make one great, but no one has been considered great who was not unique. It is by the ability to go beyond the present limits, to break the yoke of the status quo, that is essential for any who would attain greatness. It was by Abraham's willingness to leave his home and family in the greatest culture on earth, that enabled him to become one of the greatest men of all time. Abraham is the father of faith, and such is the nature of all who walk by the true faith. He went out "not knowing where he was going," but he did know what he was looking for—he was looking for what God was building, not men.

When Jesus was confronted by the Pharisees, who claimed to be "the sons of Abraham," He replied, **"If you are Abraham's children, do the deeds of Abraham" (John 8:39).** If we are the true sons of Abraham we, too, will do the deeds that he did. The present world, with all of its genius, culture, science and wealth, will not be as compelling to us as wandering in a wilderness to seek what God is doing. Those who walk by faith seldom know where they are going, but they do know exactly what they are looking for—the city which God is building. For those who have the vision, there is nothing in this life that is not worth sacrificing to walk in His purposes. We are called not only to seek what He is building, but to become a part of that building. This is the ultimate quest of man, and no man will find true satisfaction in anything else.

The church of the last days is called to greatness. We will find our greatness when we become free enough to pursue this ultimate quest. We would be hard pressed to point to any church today that was not built by men in order to attract men. There is a generation that will arise that will not build in order to attract men, but to attract God. That will be the most radical devotion to have been witnessed on earth for nearly twenty centuries. The early church turned the world upside down with its message. The last day church will turn an upside down world right side up. The spiritual generation arising will be true sons of Abraham. They will cross the barrier that the previous generations would not cross, and they will possess the Promised Land. A great demarcation is now taking place in the church. We will either be a part of the generation that perishes in the wilderness, or the one that crosses over. Having the faith to be different will be one of the distinguishing characteristics of those who cross over. ■

The Judgment Seat of Christ
Rick Joyner

THE HORDES OF HELL ARE MARCHING — Part III

Introduction

I have tried to write each section of this series as a "stand alone" message. Therefore it is not essential to have read the previous parts to benefit from this one, though it would be helpful. Also, this is written in first person because it is not fiction, but a real experience that I had. I have therefore tried to convey it just like I experienced it.

In this part I share encounters that I had with specific people before the Judgment Seat of Christ. Many of these were people that I know, or know of. I did not share their names for obvious reasons, and I would encourage you not to speculate about who they are. The point is not who they are, but the lessons that they convey.

Most prophetic dreams and visions are allegories, but this does not mean that they are not true reflections of reality. Even though this may come across like fiction, it is not, and I pray that you will take it seriously. Let the truth of the message stand as truth, and do its work in your life.

This series has become one of the most popular that we have ever published. One of the most frequent complaints that we have received about it is that you must wait three more months for the next section. I'm sorry, but there is just no way that we can remedy this if we are going to publish it in the Journal. Eventually the complete work will be published as a book that will be much more comprehensive, but I wanted to share it with you in this condensed form first. Because we feel that our Journal subscribers are a part of our family, we feel free to share things with you before we publish them for general consumption.

The Judgment Seat of Christ

I gazed one final time around the huge room inside of the mountain. The treasures of the truths of Salvation were kept here. It seemed that there was no end to their expanse or beauty. I could not imagine that the rooms which contained the other great truths of the faith could be any more glorious. This helped me to understand why so many Christians never wanted to leave this place. The large gems which represented the different aspects of Salvation all exuded a glory far beyond any earthly beauty. It was wonderful beyond description, and I knew that I could stay here for eternity and never get bored.

The eagle who was standing next to me almost shouted: "You must go on!" Then more calmly he continued, "There is no greater peace and safety than to abide in the Lord's salvation. You were brought here to know this because you will need it where you are now going. But you must not stay here any longer."

The eagle's statement about the peace and safety touched something in me. I thought about the courageous warriors who had fought in the battle from the first level of the mountain, "Salvation." They had fought so well and delivered so many, but they had also all been badly wounded. Then the eagle again interrupted my thoughts as if he were listening to them.

"God has a different definition of peace and safety than we do. To be wounded in the fight is a great honor. That is why the apostle Paul boasted of his beatings and stonings. There is no courage unless there is real danger. The Lord said He would go with Joshua to fight for the Promised Land, but over and over exhorted him to be strong and courageous because he was going to have to fight, and there would be dangers. It is in this way that the Lord proves those who are worthy of the Promises—they love God and His provision more than their own security. Courage is a demonstration of true faith. The Lord never promised that His way would be easy, but it would be worth it. The courage of those who fought from the level of Salvation moved the angels of heaven to esteem what God has wrought in the fallen race of men. They took their wounds in the terrible onslaught, but they did not quit, and they did not retreat. Even so, by climbing the mountain you were able to fight with an authority that ultimately freed even more souls. Many more souls will fill these rooms, to the great joy of heaven, if you go on."

I then turned and looked at the dark and forbidding door over which was written: *The Judgment Seat of Christ.* Just as warmth and peace had flooded my soul each time I looked at the great treasures of Salvation, fear and insecurity gripped me when I looked at this door. Everything in me wanted to stay in this room, and nothing in me wanted to go through that door. Again the eagle answered my thoughts.

"Before you enter the door to any great truth you will have these same feelings. You even felt that way when you entered into this room to the treasures of salvation. These fears are the result of the fall. They are the fruit of the

Tree of The Knowledge of Good and Evil. The knowledge from that tree made us all insecure and self-centered. The knowledge of good and evil makes the true knowledge of God seem fearful, when in fact every truth from above leads to an even greater peace and security. Even the judgments of God are to be desired, because all of His ways are perfect."

By now I had experienced enough to know that what seems right is often the least fruitful path, and sometimes the road to tragedy. Throughout my journey, the path on which it seemed that the most was risked was the path that lead to the greatest reward. Even so, each time it seemed that more was being risked. To make the choice to go on therefore got harder each time.

"It takes more faith to walk in the higher realms of the Spirit," the eagle stated, seeming a little more irritated. "The Lord gave us the map to His kingdom when He said, 'If you seek to save your life you will lose it, but if you will lose your life for My sake you will find it.' Those words alone can keep you on the path to the top of the mountain, and will lead you to victory in the great battle ahead. They will also help you to stand before the Judgment Seat of Christ," he added, looking toward the door.

I knew I had to go. I knew that I should remember this glorious room and the treasures of salvation, but I also knew that I should not look back to them again. I had to go on. I turned and with all of the courage I could muster, opened the door to the Judgment Seat of Christ and stepped through it. The troop of angels that had been assigned to me took positions all around the door, but did not enter.

"What's the matter? Aren't you coming?" I demanded, badly wanting the security of their company.

"Where you are going now you must go alone. We will be waiting for you on the other side."

Without responding, I turned and started walking before I could change my mind. It was the hardest thing I had ever done. I was in the most frightening darkness I had ever experienced. The most terrible fears rose up within me. Soon I began to think that I had stepped into hell itself. I thought about retreating, but when I looked back I could see nothing. The door was closed and I could not even see where it was located. Resolving that I now had to go on, I moved slowly, praying for the Lord to help me. As I did, peace began to grow in my heart.

I then noticed that the dark was no longer cold, but began to feel comfortable. Then I started to behold a dim light. Gradually it became a glorious light so wonderful that I felt that I was entering into heaven itself. Now the glory increased with every step. I wondered how anything this wonderful could have an entrance so dark and forbidding. I wanted to savor every step before taking another.

Soon the path opened into a hall so large that I felt that the earth itself could not contain it. The beauty of it could not even be imagined by human architects. I had never experienced anything like what filled my soul as I beheld this room. At the far end was the Source of the glory that emanated from everything else in the room. I knew that it was the Lord, and I was a little bit afraid as I began to walk toward Him. I did not even think about how great the distance was. It was all so wonderful that I felt that I could walk forever and enjoy every step. In earthly terms, that somehow did not relate here, it would have taken me many days to reach the throne.

My eyes were so fixed on the glory of the Lord that I had walked a long time before I noticed that I was passing multitudes of people who were standing in ranks to my left (there were just as many to my right but they were so far away that I did not notice them until I reached the throne). As I looked at them I had to stop. They were dazzling, more regal than anyone I had ever seen. Their countenance was captivating. Never had such peace and confidence graced a human face. Each one was beautiful beyond any earthly comparison. As I turned toward those who were close to me they bowed in a greeting as if they knew me.

"How is it that you know me?" I asked, surprised at my own boldness to ask such a question of them.

"You are one of the saints who is fighting in the last battle," a man close by responded. "Everyone here knows you, and all of those who are now fighting on the earth. We are the saints who have served the Lord in the generations before you. We are the great cloud of witnesses who have been given the right to behold the last battle. We know all of you, and we see all that you do."

I then noticed someone I had known on earth. He had been a faithful believer, but I did not think he had ever done anything of significance. He was so physically unattractive on earth that it had made him shy. Here he had the same features, but was somehow more handsome than any person I had known on earth. He stepped up to me with an assurance and dignity that I had never seen in him, or anyone, before.

"Heaven is much greater than we could have dreamed while on earth," he began. "This room is but the threshold of realms of glory that are far beyond the ability we had to comprehend. It is also true that the second death is much more terrible than we understood. Neither heaven or hell are like we thought they were. If I had known on earth what I know here I would not have lived the way that I did. You are blessed with a great grace to have come here before you have died," he said while looking at my garments.

I then looked at myself. I still had the old mantle of humility on, with the armor under it. I felt both foul and crude standing before those who were so regal and beautiful. I began to think that I was in serious trouble if I was going to appear before the Lord like this. Like the eagles, my old acquaintance could understand my thoughts, and he replied to them:

"Those who come here wearing that mantle have nothing to fear. That mantle is the highest rank of honor, and it is why they all bowed to you while you passed."

"I did not notice anyone bowing to me," I replied, a bit disconcerted.

"It is not improper," he continued. "Here we show each other the respect that is due. Even the angels serve us here, but only our God and His Christ are worshiped."

I was still ashamed. I had to restrain myself to keep from bowing to these glorious ones, while at the same time wanting to hide myself because I looked so bad. Then I began lamenting the fact that my thoughts here were just as foolish here as they were on earth, and here everyone knew them! I felt both stained and stupid standing before these who were so awesome and pure. Again my old acquaintance responded to these thoughts.

"We have our incorruptible bodies now, and you do not. Our minds are no longer hindered by sin. We are therefore able to comprehend many times what even the greatest earthly mind can fathom, and we will spend eternity growing in our ability to understand. This is so that we can know the Father, and understand the glory of His creation. On earth you cannot even begin to understand what the least of these here know, and we are the least of those here."

"How could you be the least?" I asked with disbelief.

"There is an aristocracy here. The rewards for our earthly lives are the eternal positions that we have here. This great multitude here are those whom the Lord called 'foolish virgins.' We knew the Lord, and trusted in His cross for deliverance from damnation, but we did not really live for Him, but for ourselves. We did not keep our vessels filled with the oil of the Holy Spirit. We have eternal life, but we wasted our lives on earth."

I was really surprised by this, but I also knew that no one could lie in that place.

"The foolish virgins gnashed their teeth in the outer darkness," I protested.

"And that we did. The grief that we experienced when we understood how we had so wasted our lives was beyond any grief possible on earth. The darkness of that grief can only be understood by those who have experienced it. Such darkness is magnified when it is revealed next to the glory of the One we failed. You are standing now among the lowest rank in heaven. There is no greater fools than the ones who knows the great salvation of God, but then go on living for themselves. To come here and learn the reality of that folly is a grief beyond what an earthly soul can experience. We are those who suffered this outer darkness because of this greatest of follies."

I was still incredulous. "But you are more glorious and full of more joy and peace than I even imagined, even for those in heaven. I do not feel any remorse in you, and yet I know that here you cannot lie. This does not make sense to me."

Looking me straight in the eyes, he continued, "The Lord also loves us with a love greater than you can yet understand. Before His judgment seat I tasted the greatest darkness of soul and remorse that can be experienced. Though here we do not measure time as you do, it seemed to last for as long as my life on earth had lasted. All of my sins and follies which I had not repented of passed before me, and before all who are here. The grief of this you cannot understand until you have experienced it. I felt that I was in the deepest dungeon of hell, even as I stood before the Lord. He was resolute until my life had been completely reviewed. When I said I was sorry and asked for the mercy of His cross, He wiped away my tears and took away the great darkness. He looked at me with a love that was beyond anything that you can now understand. He gave me this robe. I no longer feel the darkness or bitterness that I knew as I stood before Him, but I remember it. Only here can you remember such things without continuing to feel the pain. A moment in the lowest part of heaven is much greater than a thousand years of the highest life on earth. Now my mourning at my folly has been turned into joy, and I know that I will know joy forever, even if I am in the lowest place in heaven."

I began to think again of the treasures of salvation. Somehow I knew that all that this man had told me was revealed by those treasures. Every step I had taken up the mountain, or into it, had revealed that His ways are both more fearful and more wonderful than I had known before.

Looking at me intently, my former acquaintance continued. "You are not here to understand, but to experience. The next level of rank here is many times greater than what we have. Each level after is that much greater than the previous one. It is not just that each level has an even more glorious spiritual body, but that each level is closer to the throne where all of the glory comes from. Even so, I no longer feel the grief of my failure. I really deserve nothing. I am here by grace alone, and I am so thankful for what I have. He is so worthy to be loved. I could be doing many wondrous things now in the different realms of heaven, but I would rather stay here and just behold His glory, even if I am on the outer fringes."

Then, with a distant look in his eyes, he added, "Everyone in heaven is now in this room to watch His great mystery unfold, and to watch those of you who will fight the last battle."

"Can you see Him from here?" I asked. "I see His glory far away, but I cannot see Him."

"I can see many times better than you can," he answered. "And yes, I can see Him, and all that He is doing, even from here. I can also hear Him. I can also behold the earth. He gave us all that power. We are the great cloud of witnesses who are beholding you."

He departed back into the ranks and I began walking again, trying to understand all that he had said to me. As I looked over the great host that he had said were the foolish virgins, the ones who had spiritually slept away their life on earth, I knew that if any one of them appeared on earth now that they would be worshiped as gods, and yet they were the very least of those who were here!

I then began to think of all of the time that I had wasted in my life. It was such an overwhelming thought that I stopped. Then parts of my life began to pass before me. I began to experience a terrible grief over this one sin. I too had been one of the greatest of fools! I may have kept more oil in my lamp than others, but now I knew how foolish I had been to measure what was required of me by how others were doing. I, too, was one of the foolish virgins!

Just when I thought I would collapse under the weight of this terrible discovery, a man who I had known and esteemed as one of the great men of God I had known, came forward to steady me. Somehow his touch revived me. He then greeted me warmly. He was a man that I had wanted to be discipled by. I had met him, but we did not get along well. Like a number of others I had tried to get close enough to learn from, I was an irritation to him and he finally asked me to leave. For years I had felt guilty about this, feeling that I had missed a great opportunity because of some flaw in my character. Even though I had put it out of my mind, I still carried the weight of this failure. When I saw him it all surfaced, and a sick feeling came over me. Now he was so regal that I felt even more repulsive and embarrassed by my poor state. I wanted to hide but there was no way I could avoid him here. To my surprise, his warmth toward me was so genuine that he quickly put me at ease. There did not seem to be any barriers between us. In fact, the love I felt coming from him almost completely took away my self-consciousness.

"I have waited eagerly for this meeting," he said.

"You were waiting for me?" I asked. "Why?"

"You are just one of many that I am waiting for. I did not understand until my judgment that you were one that I was called to help, to even disciple, but I rejected you."

"Sir," I protested. "It would have been a great honor to be discipled by you, and I am very thankful for the time that I did have with you, but I was so arrogant I deserved your rejection. I know that my rebellion and pride has kept me from ever having a real spiritual father. This was not your fault, but mine."

"It is true that you were prideful, but that is not why I was offended with you. I was offended because of my insecurity, which made me want to control everyone around me. I was offended that you would not accept everything that I said without questioning it. I then started to look for anything that was wrong with you to justify my rejection. I began to feel that if I could not control you that you would one day embarrass me and my ministry. I esteemed my ministry more than I did the people for whom it was given to me, so I drove many like you away," he said.

With a genuineness that is unknown in the realms of earth, he continued, "All children are rebellious. They are all self-centered, rebellious, and think that the world revolves around them. That is why they need parents to raise them. Almost every child will at times bring reproach on his family, but he is still a part of the family. I turned away many of God's own children that he had entrusted to me for getting them safely to maturity. I failed with most of them. Most of them suffered terrible wounds and failures that I could have helped them to avoid. Many of them are now prisoners of the enemy. I built a large organization, and had considerable influence in the church, but the greatest gifts that the Lord trusted to me were the ones who were sent to me for discipline, many of whom I rejected. Had I not been so self-centered and concerned with my own reputation I would be a king here. I was called to one of the highest thrones. All that you have and will accomplish would have been in my heavenly account as well. Instead, much of what I gave my attention to was of very little true eternal significance. What looks good on earth looks very different here. What will make you a king on earth will often be a stumbling block to keep you from being a king here. What will make you a king here is lowly and unesteemed on earth. Will you forgive me?"

"Of course," I said, quite embarrassed. "But I, too, am in need of your forgiveness. I still think that it was my awkwardness and rebellion that made it difficult for you."

"It is true that you were not perfect, and I discerned some of your problems rightly, but that is never cause for rejection," he replied. The Lord did not reject the world when He saw its failures. He did not reject me when He saw my sin. He laid down His life for us. It is always the greater who must lay down his life for the lessor. I was more mature. I had more authority than you, but I became like one of the goats in the parable; I rejected the Lord by rejecting you and the others that He sent to me."

As he talked, his words were striking me deeply. I, too, was guilty of everything that he was repenting of. Many young men and women who I had brushed off as not being important enough for my time were now passing through my mind. How desperately I wanted to return now and gather them together! This grief that I began to feel was even worse than I had felt about wasting my time. I had wasted people! Now many of these were prisoners of the enemy, wounded and captured during the battle on the mountain. This whole battle was for people, and yet people were often regarded as the least important. We will fight for truths more than for the people for whom they are given. We will fight for ministries while running roughshod over the people in them. "And many people think of me as a spiritual leader! I am truly the least of the saints," I thought to myself.

"I understand how you feel," remarked another man I recognized as one I considered one of the greatest Christian leaders of all time. "Paul the apostle said near the end of his life that he was the least of the saints. Then just before his death he even called himself 'the greatest of sinners.' Had he not learned that in his life on earth he, too, would have been in jeopardy of being one of the least of the saints in heaven. Because he learned it on earth he is now one of those closest to the Lord, and will be one of the highest in rank for all of eternity."

Seeing this man in the company of "the foolish virgins" was the greatest surprise I had yet. "I cannot believe that you, too, are one of the foolish who slept away their lives on earth. Why are you here?"

"I am here because I made one of the most grave mistakes you can make as one entrusted with the glorious gospel of our Savior. Just as the apostle Paul progressed from not considering himself inferior to the greatest apostles, to being the greatest of sinners, I took the opposite course. I started out knowing that I had been one of the greatest of sinners who had found grace, but ended up thinking that I was one of the greatest apostles. It was because of my great pride, not insecurity like our friend here, that I began to attack everyone who did not see everything just the way I did. Those who followed me I stripped of their own callings, and even their personalities, pressuring them to all become just like me. No one around me could be themselves. No one dared to question me because I would crush them into powder; I thought that by making others smaller I made myself larger. I thought that I was supposed to be the Holy Spirit to everyone. From the outside my ministry looked like a smooth running machine where everyone was in unity and there was perfect order, but it was the order of a concentration camp. I took the Lord's own children and made them automatons in my own image instead of His. In the end I was not even serving the Lord, but the idol I had built to myself. By the end of my life I was actually an enemy of the true gospel, at least in practice, even if my teachings and writings seemed impeccably biblical."

"If that is true, that you became an enemy of the gospel, how is it that you are still here?" I questioned.

"By the grace of God, I did trust in the cross for my own salvation, even though I actually kept other men from it, leading them to myself rather than to Him. The Lord remains faithful to us even when we are unfaithful. It was also by his grace that the Lord took me from the earth sooner than He would have just so those who were under me could find Him and come to know Him."

I could not have been more stunned to think that this was true of this particular man. History had given us a very different picture of him. Reading what was going on in my heart, he continued:

"God does have a different set of history books than those on the earth. You have had a glimpse of this, but you do not yet know how different they are. Earthly histories will pass away, but the books that are kept here will last forever. If you can rejoice in what heaven is recording about your life, you are blessed indeed. Men see through a glass darkly, so their histories will always be clouded, and sometimes completely wrong. Very few, even very few Christians, have the true gift of discernment. Without this gift it is impossible to accurately discern truth in those of the present or the past. Even with this gift it is difficult. Until you have been here, and been stripped, you will judge others through distorted prejudices, either positive or negative. That is why we were warned not to judge before the time. Until we have been here we just cannot really know what is in the heart of others, whether they are performing good or evil deeds. There have been good motives in even the worst of men, and evil motives in even the best of them. Only here can men be judged by both their deeds and their motives."

"When I return to earth, will I be able to discern history accurately because I have been here?"

"You are here because you prayed for the Lord to judge you severely, to correct you ruthlessly, so that you could serve Him more perfectly. This was one of the most wise requests you ever made. The wise judge themselves lest they be judged. The even wiser ask for the judgments of the Lord, because they realize that they cannot even judge themselves very well. Having come here you will leave with far more wisdom and discernment, but on earth you will always see through a glass darkly to at least some degree. Your experience here will help you to know men better, but only when you are fully here can you know them fully. When you leave here you will be more impressed by how little you know men rather than by how well you know them. This is just as true in relation to the histories of men. I have been allowed to talk with you because I have in a sense discipled you through my writings, and to know the truth about me will help you greatly," the great Reformer concluded.

Then a woman stepped forward who I did not know. Her beauty and grace was breathtaking, but it was not sensual, or seductive in any way. She was the very definition of dignity and nobility.

"I was his wife on earth," she began. "Much of what you know of him actually came from me, therefore what I am about to say is not just about him, but about us. You can reform the church without reforming your own soul. You can dictate the course of history, and yet not do the Father's will, or glorify His Son. If you commit yourself to making human history, you may do it, but it is a fleeting accomplishment that will evaporate like a wisp of smoke."

"But your husband's work, or your work, greatly impacted every generation after him for good. It is hard to imagine how dark the world would have been without him," I protested.

"True. But you can gain the whole world and still loose your own soul. Only if you keep your own soul pure can you impact the world for the truly lasting eternal purposes of God. My husband lost his soul to me, and he only gained it at the end of his life because I was taken from the earth so that he could. Much of what he did he did more for me than for the Lord. I pressured him, and even gave him much of the knowledge that he taught. I used him as an extension of my own ego, because as a woman at the time I could not be recognized as a spiritual leader myself. I took over his life so that I could live my life through Him. Soon I had him doing everything just to prove himself to me."

"You must have loved her very much," I said looking at him.

"No. I did not love her at all. Neither did she love me. In fact, after just a few years of marriage we did not even like each other. But we both needed each other, so we found a way to work together. The more successful we became in this way, the more unhappy we became, and the more deception we used to fool those who followed us. We were empty wretches by the end of our lives. The more influence that you gain by your own self-promotion, the more striving you must do to keep your influence, and the more dark and cruel your life will become. Kings feared us, but we feared everyone from the kings to the peasants. We could trust no one because we were living in such deception ourselves we did not even trust each other. We preached love and trust, because we wanted everyone to love and trust us, but we feared and secretly despised everyone ourselves. If you preach the greatest truths but do not live them, you are only the greatest hypocrite."

Their words began to pound me like a hammer. I could see that already my life was heading in the same direction. How much was I doing to promote myself rather than Christ. I began to see how much I did just to prove myself to others, especially those who disliked me, or who I felt in competition with in some way. I began to see how much of my own life was built on the facades of a projected image that belied who I really was. But here I could not hide. This great cloud of witnesses all knew who I was beyond the veil of my projected motives.

I looked again at this couple. They were now so guileless and so truly noble that it was impossible to question their motives. They were gladly exposing their most devious sins for my sake, and were genuinely glad to be able to do it.

"I may have had a wrong concept of you by your history and your writings, but I have even more esteem for you now. I pray that I can carry from this place the integrity and freedom that you have now. I am tired of trying to live up to projected images of myself. How I long for that freedom." I lamented, wanting desperately to remember every detail of this encounter. Then the famous Reformer offered a final exhortation:

"Do not try to teach others to do what you are not doing yourself. Reformation is not just a doctrine. True reformation only comes from union with the Savior. When you are yoked with Christ, carrying the burdens that He gives you, He will be with you and carry them for you. You can only do His work when you are doing it with Him, not just for Him. Only the Spirit can beget that which is Spirit. If you are yoked with Him you will do nothing for the sake of politics or history. Anything that you do because of political pressures, or opportunities, will only lead you to the end of your true ministry. The things that are done for the sake of trying to make history will at best doom your accomplishments to history, and you will fail to impact eternity. If you do not live what you preach to others you disqualify yourself from the high calling of God, just as we did. I will tell you what will keep you on the path of life—love the Savior and seek His glory alone. Everything that you do to exalt yourself will one day bring you the most terrible humiliation. Everything that you do out of true love for the Savior, to glorify His name, will extend the limits of His eternal kingdom, and ultimately result in a much higher place for yourself. Live for what is recorded here. Care nothing for what is recorded on earth."

As they walked away I was again being overwhelmed by my own sin. The times that I had used people for my own purposes, or even used the glorious name of Jesus, to further my own ambitions, or to make myself look better, began to cascade down upon me. Here, where I could behold the power and glory of the One I had so used, it became more repulsive than I thought I could stand. I fell on my face in the worst despair I had ever known. After what seemed like an eternity of seeing these people and events pass before me, I felt the woman lifting me to my feet again. I was overcome by her purity, especially as I now felt so evil and corrupt. I had the strongest desire to worship her because she was so pure.

"Turn to the Son," she said emphatically. "Your desire to worship me, or anyone else at this time, is only an attempt to turn the attention away from yourself, and justify yourself by serving what you are not. I am pure now because I turned to Him. You need to see the corruption that is in your own soul, but then you must not dwell on yourself, or seek to justify yourself with dead works, but turn to Him."

This was said in such genuine love and concern that it was impossible to be hurt or offended by it. When she saw that I understood, she continued:

"The purity that you saw in me was what my husband first saw in me when we were young. I was relatively pure in my motives then, but I corrupted his love and my own purity by letting him worship me wrongly. You can never become pure just by worshiping one who is more pure than you, but only by going beyond them to find for yourself the One who has made them pure, and in Whom alone there is no sin. The more people praised us, and the more we accepted their praises, the further we departed from the path of life. Then we started living for the praises of men, and to gain power over those who would not praise us. That was our demise, and was the same for many who are here in the lowest place, but were called to be in the highest."

Wanting to simply prolong our conversation, I asked the next thing that came to my mind, "Is it difficult for you and your husband to be here together?"

"Not at all. All of the relationships that you have on earth are continued here, and they are all purified by the judgment. The more that you are forgiven the more that you love. Of course, the Lord forgave us more than anyone, and here we all love Him much more than anyone else. After we forgave each other we loved each other more. Now our relationship is continuing in much greater depth and richness because we are joint heirs of this salvation. As deep as the wounds went, that is how deep the love was able to go once we were healed. We could have experienced this on earth, but we did not learn forgiveness in time. If we had learned forgiveness the competition that entered our relationship, and sidetracked our life, would not have been able to take root in us. If you truly love, you will easily forgive. The harder it is for you to forgive, the further you are from true love. Forgiveness is essential if you are to stay on the path of life. Without it many things can knock you off the course chosen for you."

At the same time I realized that this woman, who had brought me into this confrontation with such pain at my depravity, was also the most attractive person I could ever remember meeting. It was not romantic attraction, but I just did not want to leave her. Perceiving my thoughts, she withdrew a step, indicating that she was about to go, but offered me one last insight.

"The pure truth, spoken in pure love, will always attract. You will remember the pain you feel here, and it will help you through the rest of your life. Pain is good; it shows you where there is a problem. Do not try to reduce the pain until you find and address the problem. God's truth often brings pain as it highlights a problem that we have, but His truth will always show us the way to freedom, and true life. When you know this you will even begin to rejoice in your trials, which are all allowed to help keep you on the path of life."

"Also, your attraction to me is not out of order. It is the attraction between male and female that was given in the beginning, which is always pure in its true form. When pure truth is combined with pure love, men can be the men they were created to be without having to dominate out of insecurity. Women can be the women they were created to be because their love has replaced their fear. Love will never manipulate or try to control out of insecurity, because love casts out all fear. The very place where relationships can be the most corrupted is also where they can be the most fulfilling. As your mind is renewed by the Spirit of Truth, you will not see relationships as an opportunity to get from others, but to give. Giving is the greatest fulfillment that we can ever know. It is a taste of heaven where we give to the Lord in pure worship, which has an ecstasy that even the most wonderful relationships on earth are but a fleeting glimpse of. What we experience in worship here your frail little unglorified body could not endure. The true worship of God will purify the soul for the glories of true relationships. Therefore, you must not seek relationships, but true worship. Only then can relationships start to be what they are supposed to be. True love never seeks the upper hand, but the lowest place of service. If my husband and I had kept this in our marriage, we would be sitting next to the King now, and this great hall would be filled with many more souls."

With that she disappeared back into the ranks of the glorified saints. I looked again towards the throne and the glory that appeared so much more beautiful that I was taken aback. Another man standing close to me explained:

"With each encounter, a veil is being removed so that you can see Him more clearly. You are not changed just by seeing His glory, but by seeing it with an unveiled face. Everyone who comes to the true judgments of God walks a corridor such as this to meet those who can help them remove whatever veils they are still wearing; veils that will distort their vision of Him."

I had already absorbed more understanding than I felt like my many years of study on earth had given me. I then began to feel that all of my study and seeking on earth had only lead me forward at a snail's pace. How could many lifetimes prepare me for the judgment? My life had already disqualified me more than all of those whom I had met, and they had barely made it here!

Then another man emerged from the ranks. He had been a contemporary of mine, and I did not know that he had died. I had never met him on earth, but he had a great ministry which I respected very much. Through men that he had trained, thousands had been led to salvation, and many great churches had been raised up. He asked if he could just embrace me for a minute, and I agreed, feeling a bit awkward. When we embraced I felt such love coming from him that a great pain that was deep within me stopped hurting. I had become so used to the pain that I did not even notice it until it stopped. After he released me I told him that his embrace had healed me of something. His joy at this was profound. Then he began to tell me why he was in the lowest rank in heaven.

"I became so arrogant near the end of my life that I could not imagine that the Lord would do anything of significance unless He did it through me. I began to touch the Lord's anointed, and do His prophets harm. I was selfishly proud when the Lord used one of my own disciples, and I became jealous when the Lord moved through anyone who was outside of my own ministry. I would search for anything that was wrong with them which I could attack. I did not know that every time I did this I only demoted myself further."

"I never knew that you had done anything like that," I said, surprised.

"I incited men under me to investigate others and do my dirty work. I had them scour the earth to find any error or sin in the life of others to expose them. I became the worst thing that a man can become on the earth—a stumbling block who produced other stumbling blocks. We sowed fear and division throughout the church, all in the name of protecting the truth. In my self-righteousness I was headed for perdition. In His great mercy the Lord allowed me to be struck by a disease that would bring about a slow and humiliating death. Just before I died I came to my senses and repented. I am just thankful to be here at all. I may be one of the least of His here, but it is much more than I deserve. I just could not leave this room until I had a chance to apologize to those of you that I so wronged."

"But you never wronged me," I said.

"Oh, but I did indeed," he replied. "Many of the attacks that came against you were from those whom I had agitated and encouraged in their assaults on others. Even though I may not have personally carried the attacks out, the Lord holds me as responsible as those who did."

"I see. Certainly I forgive you."

I was already beginning to remember how I had done this same thing, even if on a smaller scale. I recalled how I had allowed disgruntled former members of a church to spread their poison about that church without stopping them. I knew that by just allowing them to do this without correcting them I had encouraged them to continue. I remember thinking that this was justified because of the errors of that church. I then began to remember how I had even repeated many of their stories, justifying it by saying it was only to enlist prayers for them. Soon a great flood of other such incidents began to arise in my heart. Again, I was starting to be overwhelmed by the evil and darkness of my own soul.

"I, too, have been a stumbling block!" I wailed, dropping again to my knees. I knew that I deserved death, that I deserved the worst kind of hell. I had never seen such ruthlessness and cruelty as I was now seeing in my own heart.

"And we always comforted ourselves by actually thinking that we were doing God a favor when we attacked His own children," came the understanding voice of this man. "It is good for you to see this here, because you can go back. Please warn my disciples of their impending doom if they do not repent. Many of them are called to be kings here, but if they do not repent they will face the worst judgment of all—that of the stumbling blocks. My humbling disease was grace from God. When I stood before the throne I asked the Lord to send such grace to my disciples. I cannot cross back over to them, but He has allowed me this time with you. Please forgive and release those who have attacked you. They really do not understand that they are doing the work of the Accuser. Thank you for forgiving me, but please also forgive them. It is in your power to retain sins or cover them with love. I entreat you to love those who are now your enemies."

J could hardly hear this man I was so overwhelmed with my own sin. This man was so glorious, pure and obviously now had powers that were not known on the earth. Yet, he was entreating me with a greater humility than I had witnessed before. I felt such love coming from him that I could not imagine refusing him, but even without the impact of his love, I felt far more guilty than anyone could possibly be who was attacking me.

"Certainly I must deserve anything they have done to me, and much more," I replied.

"That is true, but it is not the point here," he entreated. "Everyone on earth is deserving of the second death, but our Savior brought us grace and truth. If we are to do His work we must do everything in both grace and truth. Truth without grace is what the enemy brings when he comes as an 'angel of light.'"

"If I can be delivered from this maybe I will be able to help them," I replied. "But can't you recognize that I am far worse than they could possibly be?"

"I know that what just passed through your mind was bad," he answered, but with a love and grace that was profound. I knew that he had now become as concerned for me and my condition as he had been for his own disciples.

"This really is heaven," I blurted out. "This really is light and truth. How could we who live in such darkness become so proud, thinking that we know so much about God? Lord!" I yelled in the direction of the throne, "Please let me go and carry this light back to earth!"

Immediately the entire host of heaven seemed to stand at attention, and I knew that I was the center of their attention. I felt so insignificant before just one of these glorious ones, but when I knew they were all looking at me, fear came like a tidal wave. I felt that there could be no doom like I was about to experience. I felt like the greatest enemy of the glory and truth that so filled that place. I was too corrupted, I could never properly represent such glory and truth. There was no way that I could in my corruption convey the reality of that glorious place and Presence. I was sure that even Satan had not fallen as far as I had from grace. This is hell I thought. There can be no worse pain than to be as evil as I am and to know that this kind of glory exists. To be banned from here is a torture worse than I ever dreamed. No wonder the demons are so angry and demented, I thought.

Just when I felt that I was about to be sent to the deepest regions of hell, I simply cried, "JESUS!" Quickly a peace came over me. I knew I had to move on toward the glory again, and somehow I had the confidence to do it. I kept moving until I saw a man who I considered one of the greatest writers of all time. I had considered his depth of insight into the truth to be possibly the greatest that I had encountered in all of my studies.

"Sir, I have always looked forward to this meeting," I almost blurted out.

"As have I," he replied with genuine sincerity.

"I feel that I know you, and in your writings I almost felt like you somehow knew me. I think that I owe more to you than to anyone else who was not canonized in Scripture," I continued.

"You are very gracious," he replied. "But I am sorry that I did not serve you better. I was a shallow person, and my writings were shallow, and filled with more worldly wisdom than divine truth."

"Since I have been here, and learned all that I have learned, I know that this must be true, but I still think they are some of the best that we have on earth," I answered.

"You are right," this famous writer admitted, with sincerity. "It is so sad. Everyone here, even those who sit closest to the King, would live their lives differently if they had them to live over, but I think that I would live mine even more differently than most. I was honored by kings, but failed the King of kings. I used the great gifts and insights that were given to me to draw men more to myself and my wisdom than to Him. Besides, I only knew Him by the hearing of the hear, which is the way I compelled other men to know Him. I made them dependent on me, and others like me. I turned

them more to deductive reasoning than to the Holy Spirit, Who I hardly knew. I did not point men to Jesus, but to myself and others like me who pretended to know Him. When I beheld Him here, I wanted to ground my writings into powder, just as Moses did to the golden calf. My mind was my idol, and I wanted everyone to worship my mind with me. Your esteem for me does not cause me to rejoice. If I had spent as much time seeking to know Him as I did seeking to know about Him in order to impress others with my knowledge, many of those who are in this lowest of companies would be sitting in the throne that was prepared for them, and many others would be in this room."

"I know by being here that your appraisal of your work is true, but are you not being a little too hard on yourself?" I questioned. "Your works fed me spiritually for many years, as I know they have multitudes of others."

"I am not being too hard on myself. All that I have said is true as it was confirmed when I stood before the throne. I produced a lot, but I was given more talents than almost anyone here, and I buried them beneath my own spiritual pride and ambitions. Just as Adam could have carried the whole human race into a most glorious future, but by his failure led billions of souls into the worst of tragedies, with authority comes responsibility. The more authority you are given, the more potential for both good and evil you will have. Those who will rule with Him for the ages will know responsibility of the most profound kind. No man stands alone, and every human failure, or victory, resonates far beyond our comprehension, even to generations to come. The many thousands who I could have led properly would have resulted in many more millions here. Anyone who understands the true nature of authority would never seek it, but only accept it when they know they are yoked with the Lord, the only One who can carry authority without stumbling. Never seek influence for yourself, but only seek the Lord and be willing to take His yoke. My influence did not feed your heart, but rather your pride in knowledge."

"How can I know that I am not doing the same?" I asked as I began to think of my own writings.

"Study to show yourself approved unto God, *not men*," he replied as he walked back into the ranks. Before he disappeared he turned and with the slightest smile, offered one last bit of advice: "And do not follow me."

In this first multitude I saw many other men and women of God from both my own time and history. I stopped and talked to many more. I was continually shocked that so many who I expected to be in the highest positions were in the lowest rank of the kingdom. Many shared the same basic story—they all had fallen to the deadly sin of pride after their great victories, or fallen to jealousy when other men were anointed as much as they were. Others had fallen to lust, discouragement, or bitterness near the end of their lives and had to be taken before they crossed the line into perdition. They all gave me the same warning: the higher the spiritual authority that you walk in, the further you can fall if you depart from love and humility.

As I continued toward the judgment seat I began to pass those who were of higher rank in the kingdom. After many more veils had been stripped away from me by meetings with those who had stumbled over the same problems that I had, I began to meet those who had overcome. I met couples who had served the Lord and each other faithfully to the end. Their glory here was unspeakable, and their victory encouraged me that it was possible to stay on the path of life, and serve Him in faithfulness. Those who stumbled, stumbled in many different ways. Those who prevailed all did it the same way—they did not deviate from their devotion to the first and greatest commandment—loving the Lord. By this their service was done unto Him, not men, not even for spiritual men. These were the ones who worshipped the Lamb, and followed Him wherever He went.

When I was still not even half way to the throne, what had been the indescribable glory of the first rank now seemed to be the outer darkness in comparison to the glory of those I was now passing. The greatest beauty on earth would not qualify to be found anywhere in heaven. And I was told that this room was just the threshold of realms indescribable!

My march to the throne may have taken days, months or even years. There was no way to measure time in that place. To my considerable discomfort, they all showed great respect to me, not because of who I was or anything that I had done, but simply because I was a warrior in the battle of the last days. Somehow, through this last battle, the glory of God would be revealed in such a way that it would be a witness to every power and authority, created or yet to be created, for all of eternity. During this battle the glory of the cross would be revealed, and the wisdom of God would be known in a special way. To be in that battle was to be given one of the greatest honors given to those of the race of men.

As I approached the Judgment Seat of Christ, those in the highest ranks were also sitting on thrones that were all a part of His throne. Even the least of these thrones was more glorious than any earthly throne many times over. Some of these were rulers over cities on earth who would soon take their place. Others were rulers over the affairs of heaven, and others over the affairs of the physical creation, such as star systems and galaxies. However, it was apparent that those who were given authority over cities were esteemed above those who had even been given authority over galaxies. The value of a single child was more than a galaxy of stars, because the Holy Spirit dwelt in men, and the Lord had chosen men as His eternal dwelling place. In the presence of His glory the whole earth seemed as insignificant as a speck of dust, and yet was so infinitely esteemed that the attention of the whole host of heaven was upon it.

Now that I stood before the throne, I felt very much less than a speck of dust. Even so, I felt the Holy Spirit upon me in a greater way than I ever had. It is was by His power alone that I was able to stand. It was here that I truly came to understand His ministry as our Comforter. He had led me through the entire journey even though I had hardly noticed Him.

The Lord was both more gentle and more terrible than I had ever imagined. In Him I saw Wisdom who had accompanied me up the mountain, and felt the familiarity of many of my friends on earth. I recognized Him as the One I had heard speaking to me many times through others. I also recognized Him as the One that I had often rejected when He had come to me in others. I saw both a Lion and a Lamb, the Shepherd and the Bridegroom, but most of all I saw Him here as the Judge.

Even in His awesome presence, the Comforter was so mightily with me I was comfortable. It was also apparent that the Lord in no way wanted me to be uncomfortable; He only wanted me to know the truth. Human words are not adequate to describe either how awesome, or how relieving it was to stand before the Lord. I had passed the point where I was concerned if the judgment was going to be good or bad; I just knew it would be right, and that I could trust my Judge.

At one point the Lord looked toward the galleries of thrones around Him. Many were occupied by saints, and many were empty. He then said, "These thrones are for the overcomers who have served Me faithfully in every generation. My Father and I prepared them before the foundation of the world. Are you worthy to sit in one of these?"

I remembered what a friend had once said, "When an omniscient God asks you a question, it is not because He is seeking information." I looked at the thrones. I looked at those who were now seated. I could recognize some of the great heros of the faith, but most of those seated I knew had not even been well known on earth. Many I knew had been missionaries who had expended their lives in obscurity. They had never cared to be remembered on earth, but only to Him. I was a bit surprised to see some who had been wealthy, or rulers who had been faithful with what they had been given. However, it seemed that faithful, praying women and mothers occupied more thrones than any other single group.

There was no way that I could answer "yes" to the Lord's question if I considered myself worthy to sit here. I was not worthy to sit in the company of any who were there. I knew I had been given the opportunity to run for the greatest prize in heaven or earth, and I had failed. I was desperate, but there was still one hope. Even though most of my life had been a failure, I knew that I was here before I had finished my life on earth. When I confessed that I was not worthy, He asked:

"But do you want this seat?"

"I do with all of my heart," I responded.

The Lord then looked at the galleries and said, "Those empty seats could have been filled in any generation. I gave the invitation to sit here to everyone who has called upon My name. They are still available. Now the last battle has come, and many who are last shall be first. These seats will be filled before the battle is over. Those who will sit here you will know by two things: they will wear the mantle of humility, and they will have My likeness. You now have the mantle. If you can keep it and do not lose it in the battle, when you return you will also have My likeness. Then you will be worthy to sit with these, because I will have made you worthy. All authority and power has been given to Me, and I alone can wield it. You will prevail, and you

will be trusted with My authority only when you have come to fully abide in Me. Now turn and look at My household."

I turned and looked back in the direction I had come from. From before His throne I could see the entire room. The spectacle was beyond any earthly comparison for its glory. Millions filled the ranks. Each individual in the lowest rank was more awesome than an army, and I knew had more power. It was far beyond my capacity to absorb such a panorama of glory. Even so, I could see that only a very small portion of the great room was occupied.

I then looked back at the Lord and was astonished to see tears in His eyes. He had wiped the tears away from every eye here, but His own. As a tear ran down His cheek he caught it in His hand. He then offered it to me.

"This is My cup. Will you drink it with Me?"

There was no way that I could refuse Him. As the Lord continued to look at Me I began to feel His great love. Even as foul as I was He still loved me. As undeserving as I was He wanted me to be close to Him. Then He said:

"I love all of these with a love that you cannot now understand. I also love all who are supposed to be here but did not come. I have left the ninety nine to go after the one who was lost. My shepherds would not leave the one to go after the ninety nine who are still lost. I came to save the lost. Will you share My heart to go to save the lost? Will you help to fill this room? Will you help to fill these thrones, and every other seat in this hall?

Will you take up this quest to bring joy to heaven, to Me and to My Father? This judgment is for My own household, and My own house is not full. The last battle will not be over until My house is full. Only then will it be time for us to redeem the earth, and remove the evil from My creation. If you drink My cup you will love the lost the way that I loved them."

He then took a cup so plain that I was surprised that it even existed in a room of such glory, and He placed His tear in it. He then gave it to me. I have never tasted anything so bitter. I knew that I could in no way drink it all, or even much of it, but I was determined to drink as much as I could. The Lord patiently waited until I finally erupted into such crying that I felt like veritable rivers of tears were flowing from me. I was crying for the lost, but even more I was crying for the Lord.

I looked to Him in desperation as I could not take any more of this great pain. Then His peace began to fill me and mix with His love that I was feeling. Never had I felt anything so wonderful. This was the living water that I knew could spring up for eternity. Then I felt as if the waters flowing within me caught on fire. I began to feel that this fire would consume me if I could not begin declaring the majesty of His glory. I had never felt such an urge to preach, to worship Him, and to breathe every breath that I was given for the sake of His gospel.

"Lord!" I shouted out, forgetting everyone but Him. "I now know that this throne of judgment is also the throne of grace, and I ask You now for the grace to serve You. Above all things I ask You for grace! I ask You for the grace to finish my course. I ask You for the grace to love

You like this so that I can be delivered from the delusions and self-centeredness that so pervert my live. I call upon You for salvation from myself and the evil of my own heart, and for this love that I now feel to flow continually in my heart. I ask You to give me Your heart, Your love. I ask You for the grace of the Holy Spirit to convict me of my sin. I ask You for the grace of the Holy Spirit to testify of You, as You really are. I ask for the grace to testify of all that You have prepared for those who come to You. I ask for the grace to be upon me to preach the reality of this judgment. I ask for the grace to share with those who are called to occupy these empty thrones, to give them words of life that will keep them on the path of life, that will impart to them the faith to do what they have been called to do. Lord, I beg You for this grace."

The Lord then stood up. Then all of those who were seated upon the thrones for as far as I could see also stood up. His eyes burned with a fire I had not seen before.

"You have called upon Me for grace. This request I never deny. You shall return, and the Holy Spirit shall be with you. Here you have tasted of both My kindness and My severity. You must remember both if you are to stay on the path of life. The true love of God includes the judgment of God. You must know both my kindness and severity or you will fall to deception. This is the grace that you have been given here, to know both. The conversations you had with your brethren here were My grace. Remember them."

He then pointed His sword toward my heart, then my mouth, then my hands.

When He did this fire came from His sword and burned me with a great pain. "This too is grace," He said. "You are but one of many who have been prepared for this hour. Preach and write about all that you have seen here. What I have said to you say to My brethren. Go and call My captains to the last battle. Go and defend the poor and the oppressed, the widows and the orphans. This is the commission of My captains, and it is where you will find them. My children are worth more to Me than the stars in the heavens. Feed My lambs. Watch over My little ones. Give the word of God to them that they may live. Go to the battle. Go and do not retreat. Go quickly for I will come quickly. Obey Me and hasten the day of My coming."

A company of angels then came and escorted me away from the throne. The leader walked beside me and began to speak.

"Now that He has stood He will not sit again until the last battle is over. He has been seated until the time when His enemies are to be put under His feet. The time has now come. The legions of angels that have been standing ready since the night of His passion have now been released upon the earth. The hordes of hell have also been released. This is the time that all of creation has been waiting for. The great mystery of God will soon be finished. We will now fight until the end. We will fight with you and your brethren."

𝕵 awoke. ∎

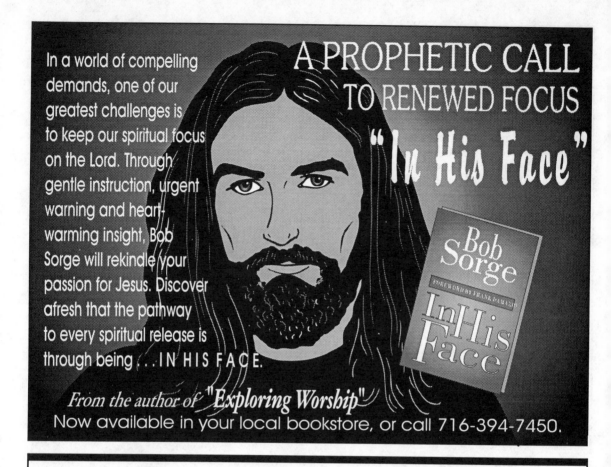
The *MorningStar Fellowship of Ministries* (MFM) was founded to serve three basic parts of the overall vision of *MorningStar*. **First** is the equipping, oversight, and support of ministries related to *Morning-Star*. **Second** is to use the relationship that *MorningStar* has with many different parts of the body of Christ to promote interchange, understanding and friendship between them. The **third** is for the mobilizing of spiritual forces for the sake of the gospel.

For additional information, or to request an application, contact:

The MorningStar Fellowship of Ministries
16000 Lancaster Highway
Charlotte, NC 28277
Phone 704-542-9880 • Fax 704-542-5763